MysteryDates®

How to keep the sizzle in your relationship

Hundreds of tips on what to do, how to do it, and where to go — locally, nationally, globally

From all over the omniverse, readers hail *MysteryDates*®

"Wow, what a lot of research went into this book! Lots of great ideas. As much a travelogue as a guide to dates."
— Michaele Ballard; Goose Creek, South Carolina

"I love this concept of *MysteryDates*. It's certainly necessary, I think, for long-term relationships — at least those that last more than a weekend! — reminding us of who we have been to each other, and who we are today."
— Linda Kosut; San Francisco, California

"What a delight to take in. This is a book that, using the exciting concepts of creativity, spontaneity, and trust, is destined to be one of the best 'relationship' books a couple might receive for a wedding present. Not to mention the incredible overview of interesting activities and places available for *MysteryDates* close to home and around the world. In a category of its own. Love it!"
— Toby Adelman, PhD, RN; Mars Hill, Maine

"Amazing! Open author Woody Weingarten's *MysteryDates* anywhere and you'll find the perfect possibility for your own surprise date with your loved one. From quirky to elegant, free to big bucks, the options abound."
— Suzan Berns; San Rafael, California

"MysteryDates were introduced to me by Woody and Nancy decades ago. My former husband and I loved the idea and happily indulged in them. They are not just for husbands and wives or committed partners. They are also a gift between close friends. The receiver experiences excitement and anticipation of a pleasant experience, and the giver experiences the joy of knowing his/her loved one will be pleasantly surprised and enjoy the experience. MysteryDates, although originating in the United States, is a global concept. They can be experienced in any part of the world, and by people living in different parts of the world. They can be experienced by any economic class since you do not need to spend any money to give someone a memorable experience. MysteryDates are highly recommended based upon my personal experience. Indulge!"
— **Georgia McDaniel; Vestiaria, Portugal**

"As long-time post-millennials on the prowl for meaning and exciting things to do with our ever-diminishing time untethered from our technologies, this is the only guide you'll need — one filled with the best event ideas you'll ever encounter."
— **Bernie Krause, Author,** *The Great Animal Orchestra*; **Sonoma, California**

"Inventive, invigorating, incisive, inspirational — the "i's" have it."
— **Suzanne Machbitz; Chandler, Arizona**

"MysteryDates are a fresh and wonderful way to spice up a relationship. Author Woody Weingarten provides dozens of ways to surprise and delight your spouse or partner. There are ideas for MysteryDates for the whole family, too. I can't wait to surprise my husband with our first one."
— **Fanny Levy; Northridge, California**

"This book is for everyone. Each chapter is filled with great ideas on how to surprise that special someone, young or old. *MysteryDates* is a guidebook to build or sustain a healthy relationship."
— **Ginny Carter; Bend, Oregon**

"*Mystery Dates* is a treasure of original and pertinent information. Any reader can use it — even if his or her date will not be mysterious. It is a great book to refer to."
— **Mike Hartl; Tiburon, California**

"Loved this book! So many great ideas for creating a lifetime of special memories. Woody Weingarten and Nancy Fox's love for each other really comes through on the pages. I found so much sage advice woven throughout the book for building a strong relationship based on trust and generosity."
— **Lea Dutton; Asheville, North Carolina**

"I enjoyed reading *MysteryDates*. Wow, what a huge number of fun ideas!"
— **Dan Newman; Berkeley, California**

"In *MysteryDates*, Woody Weingarten stumbles upon the beating heart of the Tao of randomocity, and with good humor shares his findings, for the betterment of humankind. This bracingly paced wandering meditation on the unwritten constitution of life packs in a fascinating variety of practical tips for keeping older relationships flexible, high on life, and fun, projecting folk art for the soul far and wide, from the Liberace Museum to the Idiotarod and beyond, never losing sight of its quest to reflect the great glues of meaningful relationships everywhere: trust, communication, and acceptance."
— **Carleton Cole; Author,** *Siamese Arabesques: Tales of the Islamic World with Thai Twists***; Bangkok, Thailand**

"Woody Weingarten's suggestions are alluring, erotic, and tempting, so *MysteryDates* might be just the answer to a relationship that needs an injection of life."
— **Robert Story; Laguna Beach, California**

A good book. Very amusing.
— **Dick Pollinger; Tampa, Florida**

"To survive, any long-term relationship needs to have surprises. A surprise, whether in the form of a date or a gift, takes the boredom out of life. Woody Weingarten's autobiographical summary of surprise dates he's had in the San Francisco Bay Area does exactly that. A fun-fast read and self-help guide to better understanding your significant other."
— **Jim Brown; Richmond, California**

"Woody Weingarten's new book, *MysteryDates*, offers hundreds of ideas — as well as personal anecdotes — to get you out of your house and into a world filled with possibilities. That world can add 'sizzle' to your relationship and help you rediscover the magic of your first days together. The innovation here is that one partner plans a surprise activity for the other. A MysteryDate can be almost anything, from something simple — taking out the time to watch a sunset in your own backyard garden — to boarding a plane to Hawaii to visit a volcano. Happily married for over three decades, Weingarten, who writes in his own inimitable humoristic style well known to San Francisco readers, has been, in his own words, 'concocting MysteryDates virtually from the git-go.'"
— **Roberta Bienenfeld, Editor and Translator; Ramat Beit Shemesh, Israel**

MysteryDates®

How to keep the sizzle in your relationship

Hundreds of tips on what to do, how to do it, and where to go — locally, nationally, globally

by WOODY WEINGARTEN

Author of The Roving I; Grampy and His Fairyzona Playmates; and Rollercoaster: How a man can survive his partner's breast cancer

VitalityPress

Copyright © 2024, Sherwood L. Weingarten
All rights reserved.

This book may not be reproduced in whole or in part, stored in a retrieval system, or transmitted in any form or by any means — electronic, mechanical, or other — without written permission from the publisher (woody@vitalitypress.com), except by a reviewer, who may quote brief passages in a review.

VitalityPress
VitalityPress.com

Publishing management by Ruth Schwartz, thewonderlady.com
Cover design: Joe Marciniak
Back cover photo: Michael Fox

Publisher's Cataloging-in-Publication data
(Provided by Cassidy Cataloguing Services, Inc.).

Names: Weingarten, Woody, author.

Title: MysteryDates : how to keep the sizzle in your relationship : hundreds of tips on what to do, how to do it, and where to go -- locally, nationally, globally / by Woody Weingarten.

Description: [San Anselmo, California] : VitalityPress, [2024]

Identifiers: ISBN: 978-0-9905543-9-4 (paperback) | 979-8-9892103-1-2 (hardcover) | 979-8-9892103-0-5 (ebook) | LCCN: 2023924072

Subjects: LCSH: Dating (Social customs) | Interpersonal relations. | Man-woman relationships. | Mate selection. | Travel. | Vacations. | BISAC: TRAVEL / General. | FAMILY & RELATIONSHIPS / Activities. | HUMOR / General.

Classification:
LCC: HQ801 .W45 2024 | DDC: 306.73--dc23

Dedication

I dedicate this MysteryDates® book to my father, an extraordinary guy long gone from the flesh but ever-present in spirit; to my mother, whose strength and courage I didn't recognize until shortly before my dad died; and to my exceptionally wonderful wife who's still aiding me every day of my life.

To Irving N. Weingarten, my hero and mentor, who encouraged me to strive always for excellence and to experience the whole enchilada (always within the bounds of reason), including what normally would go unseen right in front of my eyes.

To Matilda Weingarten, whose extraordinariness was hidden so long by her husband's grandeur, whose unconditional love I didn't fully accept until she was no longer there.

To Nancy Fox, my bright, talented, loyal, funny spouse, who's put up with my idiosyncrasies and human frailties for more than three decades.

—Woody Weingarten
January 2, 2024
San Anselmo, California

Table of Contents

Dedication ix

Part 1: Intro by the author 1

Part 2: Romance, intimacy, sex 7

Part 3: Special days 15

Part 4: Endless possibilities 23

Part 5: Walks 35

Part 6: Imperfectly perfect 43

Part 7: Eating 49

Part 8: For poorer or richer 57

Part 9: Sports, games 65

Part 10: Quirky 73

Part 11: Adventure 83

Part 12: Travel, tourism 91

Part 13: Spontaneity 101

Part 14: Museums 109

Part 15: Masquerading 119

Part 16: Hobbies, classes 129

Part 17: Performances 139

Part 18: Mental wellness 149

Part 19: Conversations, lectures, sermons 159

Part 20: Family 167

Part 21: Parades, festivals 177

Part 22: Book readings 185

Part 23: Discoveries 193

Part 24: Themes 203

Part 25: Fairs 'n' fun 211

Part 26: Love, love, love 217

Part 27: Diff'rent strokes 227

Part 28: Home sweet home 235

Part 29: Birds, butterflies, beasts, bits 243

Part 30: Mysteries.. 253

Part 31: Afterword 259

Thanks 265

Woody Weingarten, a bio 267

More Woody Weingarten books 269

Part 1

Intro by the author

A MysteryDate® doesn't typically entail a cloak 'n' dagger or a scruffy private eye who can't afford to shower regularly.

Nor is it likely to involve finding out what's growing in the back of your refrigerator, or whether we've been invaded by aliens from the Andromeda Galaxy.

What *is* a MysteryDate then? An activity you arrange without your partner knowing where she or he is going *until* you get there. Or vice versa — that is, one arranged with *you* in the dark.

The result can keep, resuscitate, or refresh the sizzle and joy that flared when sparks first sparked between you (as well as the fun that followed).

These dates can also clobber the myth that long-term relationships are inevitably doomed to become unexciting, monotonous, or drab. If yours has lost even a smidgeon of its oomph, however, this book might help you find the pizzazz again. Without strain.

MysteryDates, you see, can be simple or complicated, a one-shot or a series. They'll most often involve only you and your partner. But a third person or second couple might join in on occasion. Or even, conceivably, a larger group of friends, relatives, co-workers.

I — Woody Weingarten, author of this guidebook — am confident, in fact, that these events can work for nearly everyone (even if Covid, its variants, subvariants, and sub-subvariants require booster shots forever).

Yes, some novices may find their partners naturally resistant. But that initial foot-dragging is likely to dissipate, soon replaced by anticipation and excitement, once the practice has been habituated. The newbies then will joyously become MysteryDate planners themselves.

Not incidentally, I mostly refer throughout this volume to he and she because that's what Nancy Fox, my wife, and I *are*. If, however, your relationship consists of a he and a he, a she and a she, a threesome, or includes a they or two — simply substitute your words or lifestyle for mine.

Nance (that's her rhymes-with-dance nickname) and I have been happily married for well over three decades and have been concocting MysteryDates virtually from the git-go. We even scheduled them, albeit less frequently, when she was undergoing treatments for breast cancer. We did stop while the pandemic raged, but we've begun again. Completely vaxxed and boosted. Happy.

Along the way, we've imposed but one guideline: The date's originator must firmly believe the event will amuse, exhilarate, or (at worst) please the other.

A caveat: This book probably won't help much if you're on the brink of a split-up or if one of you just gave the other an SDI (Sexually Transmitted Infection) — or if you never, ever like surprises. It can, conversely, be of inordinate assistance if your prime currency is trust and you're seeking a new path to a good time.

Another caveat: I'm one person, as individual as any snowflake, so please take my advice — despite my expertise and the mountain ranges of research I did — with 17 grains of salt.

That said, doing a delight-filled date is as obvious and easy as ABC:
- A. Decide on something you're at least 93.7 percent sure you and your partner will relish.
- B. Figure out, specifically, how to make it happen.
- C. Do it.

Frequency isn't critical

With MysteryDates, you determine your own pace. And, unlike some male sexual appetites, frequency is immaterial.

One partner might pull off four or five in a row, or two in a day (I once slated three, but, frankly, Nance and I both found that number exhausting). A couple of months can zip by without even one.

At one point I became a trifle lazy and more than occasionally limited my MysteryDates to shows I could easily obtain tickets to — "lazy" and "easily" being the crucial words. Besides, I've enthusiastically found multiple online sites that offer twofers or other entertainment bargains.

The fundamental idea is to build on your individual preferences. I once took Nance to three jazz concerts in a week. You might prefer a lone ComicCon, local PTA board meeting, or annual gathering of Mensa geniuses. Or two consecutive days at 7-11 for hot dogs and Slurpees.

The length of any given date also doesn't matter. We've had quickie local lunches that ran less than an hour, and one to Las Vegas that went on for a week sandwiched between air excursions.

Perfection and pizzazz

I strongly suggest you use this volume as a "how-to" guide, to be dipped into for tips rather than read cover-to-cover in a single sitting. Perfect for the throne? Probably — just like my previous collection of newspapers columns, *The Roving I*.

Note that I haven't resurrected our San Francisco-centric and other experiences so you can mimic them. My anecdotes are meant, instead, to amuse, enlighten and, most of all, be samples that spur you to shape dates to *your* specifications, or your partner's.

Boredom, I firmly believe, need not be a word in your lexicon (unless you live Boredom, Oregon); you most likely already possess the tools you need to thrive: my written roadmaps, *your* Google, and *somebody's* GPS-type device. Plus, above all, your imagination.

Part 2, "Romance, intimacy, sex," can act as a compass. Flip forward to "Adventure," Part 11, and you'll discover more-robust choices: whitewater-rafting, bungee-jumping or, well, pick your own peril. Favor something less daunting? Skip ahead to Part 13, "Spontaneity," and avoid wrapping up every detail in advance (as in, "We're going on a MysteryDate in seven minutes").

Or you can try a date in which the clickety-clack of a train can put you to sleep, or you fly off wide-eyed to a touristy spot you've both fancied (such as the Rock and Roll Hall of Fame and Museum in Cleveland or Hilo on the Big Island in Hawaii).

Is dining out, or in, your thing? Are you into sports or games (playing, observing, betting)? Prefer to hang out in dark exhibition halls or sit in silence at string-quartet recitals or staged readings — or, maybe, go slightly wild at outdoor rock festivals? Want to immerse yourself in nature (or lectures or classes)? Have a penchant for discovering the unknown? Enjoy the weird, the quirky, the one-of-a-kind?

I cover all those and, as a circus barker might bellow, "more, lots more." With a dash of humor, I pray.

Covid forced tons of venues to close. The vast majority eventually reopened. Although I just re-investigated each reference in this book for accuracy, I still suggest you pick your must-see topic from the table of contents and triple-check that the place or event you want to visit hasn't been closed by a spanking new virus or variant in the last couple of weeks. Then, begin.

It should be that painless to replenish your pizzazz.

— **Woody Weingarten**
January 2, 2024

Part 2

Romance, intimacy, sex

I vividly remember spinning to a big band with Nancy decades ago, when time stood still for an instant and created an illusion that we were the only couple on the dance floor yet, somehow, had simultaneously left the earthly plane.

That, arguably, may have been the zenith of our 65-year romance. But we've had scads of other striking and tender memories. One of the simplest and best — especially since we not infrequently go big, bigger, and overboard — was a standard-issue, "ordinary" MysteryDate® that I'd carefully crafted for one of my wife's "no-big-number, no-big-deal" birthdays.

Basically, I stuck to basics.

But I did set our dining room table with fancier dishes than we normally use (plus real-silver utensils and candles — items we hadn't de-cobwebbed, washed, or polished in ages). And I yanked from the microwave, seconds before they burned, several of Nance's favorite foods that I'd bought at a local supermarket. Then I dimmed the lights and made sure soft dinner-jazz streamed into the room, topping it all off with daisies plucked from our yard. Along with incense from a local boutique.

The chow-down-at-home MysteryDate was especially delicious because I normally don't cook and my wife had expected she'd have to do it all that night as usual — or, only slightly better, that we'd end up going to a familiar local eatery.

My brainchild certainly was better received — despite not deviating that far from our customary home dining — than if I'd muttered, "Feel like doing anything special tonight, babe?"

Poetry and motion

Elizabeth Barrett Browning penned these everlasting poetic lines: "How do I love thee? Let me count the ways. I love thee to the depth and breadth and height my soul can reach."

Women and men alike, particularly those with sensitive or quixotic souls, undoubtedly can relate. But I also believe all genders can contentedly — and repeatedly — bask in MysteryDates that contain romance, intimacy, and/or sexuality.

Forms those elements might take are infinite, from a traditional lakeside walk under a starry, starry night to the kinkiest of kinky activities (if you truly get off on hanging from a chandelier, go for it).

Here are ways — some conventional, some atypical — that you potentially can count on for a modicum of enjoyment:

- Get up early and watch the sunrise together. Or stay up late and view a lunar eclipse.
- Re-do some activity you haven't repeated in eons but fondly remember as romantic. Such as performing karaoke at an open mic, sipping a root beer float through two straws, strolling arm-in-

arm through a mall, taking a hayride, or window-shopping for lacy undergarments.
- Appreciate the view — day or night or both — from the top floor of a skyscraper or a castle in Spain.
- Rent a hotel room close to the workplace of your husband/wife/partner and call him/her/they to meet you in Room XXX for a midday matinee. Or harmoniously cook a meal and consume it ever so slowly, nude, feeding one another the delicacies and sexy confidences.
- Spend an evening of intimacy by writing each other love poems (or prose if you can't get the meter running). Or read aloud lists you've made of traits you adore about your heartthrob. Or listen to a string of love songs.
- Rent a limo, bring your favorite apple juice or sparkling wine, and ride around for an hour or two with no destination whatsoever.
- Find a rusty oilcan and playfully inform your lover you're her/his romance genie who's escaped from it and will grant three *reasonable* wishes (a constraint that most likely disqualifies desires for either a personal Lear jet or world peace).
- Have phone sex (perhaps cell to cell) in your own home, in adjacent rooms. Make it a Zoom, WhatsApp, or FaceTime date if you require optics. Or engage in an intimate, private, two-person sex-toy party. Or read to your partner from a bodice-ripper or stroke book and be sure to exaggerate the panting and shouts of "Oh, God."
- For the ultimate romantic getaway, take a gondola ride in Venice. If Italy isn't in your near future, substitute Naples Island in Long Beach, California. A one-

hour tour there comes replete with bread and cheese.
- Anoint each other with coconut oil for the most magnificent massages ever.
- Party in Fort Lauderdale, notorious for the debauchery of consenting collegians during "spring break" when its population swells from 183,000 to more than a quarter of a million. Instead of looking for the lusty, though, you might choose to kayak in the dark or pretend you're Scarlett O'Hara and Rhett Butler, star-crossed lovers in the 1939 film classic *Gone with The Wind*, as you sup at the small and charming plantation-style Pillars Hotel there.
- Enjoy a special sip 'n' slip moment by nursing a cocktail you both cherish while washing each other's back in a tub laced with bubble-bath crystals and rose petals.
- Suggest that your mate track down the slew of loving chocolates or pink lilies or Post-it notes you've hidden throughout your home in drawers, attic and/or cellar. And then do whatever comes naturally, be it a light kiss on the forehead or a full-fledged romp on a rooftop.
- Should you believe there's romance in the crypt-ic, consider visiting the Hollywood Memorial Cemetery remains of Tinseltown's most famous silent screen lover, Rudolph Valentino, aka "The Sheik."
- Attend, together, the Masturbate-a-Thon awareness- and fund-raising festivals for participants and voyeurs that have been held (once or annually) in D.C., Oakland, Philadelphia, Portland, and San Francisco — as well as Copenhagen, London, and Montreal.
- Hold hands and fantasize out loud about your

personal dream-couple — Elvis and Priscilla Presley, let's say, while visiting the legendary singer's Graceland mansion in Memphis (or the Graceland Wedding Chapel in Las Vegas).
- Cheer-on your beloved sports franchise and sneak in a kiss or two each time there's a goal, run, touchdown, or good play.
- Park and "make out" the way you remember doing as teens, in a spot you both still salivate over, then perhaps follow up by dancing outside the car to an oldie by The Big Bopper, Boyz II Men, or The Grateful Dead that booms from your smart phone instead of your dead boombox.

What you and I *can't* do anymore (though you *can* simulate it) is attend a Cuddle-Con, an all-day "platonic touching" event that was a one-shot in 2015 run by the Cuddle Up to Me shop in Portland, Oregon. Sad, maybe, but it simply didn't touch enough people to flourish as a public event.

Nance and I, to be honest, can't do a variety of other things anymore because of the aging process and our heading deeper into geezerhood. We've both run out of youth but not the desire or ability to enjoy life to the fullest. We therefore do what we're able and never fret about the regularity (or irregularity) of our MysteryDates any more than we panic about how often we sidestep devouring the federally recommended amount of organic fruit and veggies.

I heart you, sweetie

Although annual Valentine's Days may generally generate stress and spasms because of ginormous expectations, they can instead morph into your most dreamy, amorous, extraordinary MysteryDates.

Whether you pursue, woo, or yabbadabbadoo your sweetheart on that Hallmark holiday by supplying candelabras or candies, diamonds or a trip to Diamond Head, Eggs Benedict in bed or a benediction by a Benedictine monk, it makes no difference where you live. San Francisco usually is no more inviting on any given day of celebration — like July 13, Embrace Your Geekness Day — than is Bowlegs, Oklahoma, or Peculiar, Missouri.

In our adopted hometown (population-12,336 San Anselmo, a jump, skip and hop from the Fisherman's Wharf tourist-traps so many travelers favor), our I-heart-you holiday traditionally ends with a MysteryDate but starts with discovering (almost everywhere) little sugary candy hearts with saccharine sayings.

Nance began our hide-the-heart-while-flaunting-our-love custom years ago by burying them in my briefcase, medicine cabinet, pants cuffs, and countless other locations. I copied the idea a couple of years later, substituting her bra for the cuffs and her piano bench for the briefcase. We've both been playing the game on-and-off ever since — and have found, sometimes up to five years after a hideaway, some pristine, untouched candies we suspect must have a half-life of several centuries. Longer even than Twinkies.

My wife increased the sweet's size a couple of times, presumably to show me her love had grown. And I once cut hearts out of felt, playfully proving — forgive me, dear readers — "my heart-felt feelings."

Too much trouble? Don't do it! But do express your love in your own, inimitable way. Emphasize, if you can, the romance.

Many moons ago I scribbled at length in my journal about my relationship. Here's an abridged version:

"*I first met Nancy when we were awkward, skinny, inarticulate teens. She lived in Detroit. I lived in New Rochelle, New York.*

"*We met in a pizza parlor near my home, instantly fell in love, and started 'going steady.'*

"*I gave her my fraternity pin — although she was, at age 17, very nervous about my touching her breast.*

"*But then I told her I was going to become a writer. 'I don't like starving,' she said. 'Maybe we should see some other people.'*

"*We broke up.*

"*We re-met by accident/coincidence/destiny almost three decades later in Northern California as we each ordered a diet soda at a pizzeria bar.*

"*Long story short, we got married.*"

Years later, Nance thought our serendipitous love story cool enough to be a candidate for *How We First Met*, a live interview/improv show that started in 2000 in San Francisco and spread to other cities. Before it disappeared into the ozone, my partner submitted our tale, and we were selected. She set up it up as a MysteryDate, of course.

As Jill Bourque (who'd created the event) interviewed us, she instructed the stage performers how to enact our saga in musical form, in slow motion, as a silent movie, in a bevy of other ways. With giggles and poignancy. We wish we had an audio or video recording, but the friends who accompanied us were digitally challenged and never found the right buttons.

Not to worry. We've bronzed the memory in our brains.

Part 3

Special days

Each person on the planet could probably name several personal days that could make exquisite MysteryDates® — even if they wouldn't mean diddly to anyone else.

Let's say May 18 is the day you finally got married. Why not alternate chances to venerate the occasion? Odd years, you get to plan one; even, it's your mate's turn. Or the other way around.

There's never any harm in knowing *when* a MysteryDate's going to happen; the key factor is keeping "the other" unaware of its form. Your partner might surprise you, for instance, by commemorating the day you moved into your new house, the hour you won the lottery or cashed in your inheritance, the time you found a new job (or retired), the time *and* date your child was conceived, or the day you finally were able to laugh at the poison ivy you inadvertently picked for your partner as a bouquet.

Or the minute you pledged to stop drinking or smoking, the day you graduated from grammar school or college or karate class, the afternoon you brought home the super-cute kitty (or chimp or hamster).

You may even invent a private fete, labeling it with own name and following up by celebrating Penelope's Day or Santiago's Day once a month, once a year, once a decade.

Not your cup of java juice? Well, you could choose to keep things elementary and mark *only* your partner's birthday (or her or his half-birthday — yeah, I have friends who refuse to wait an entire year to do that particular MysteryDate so they salute each other every six months).

Want to stick with traditional days? Try observing — with your do-it-yourself stamp of approval on them, of course — St. Patrick's Day, the Fourth of July, Secretary Appreciation Day, National Joe Day or National Pickle Day, Purim or a day within the 40 of Lent or the month of Ramadan that has individualized meaning for you and/or your companion.

MysteryDate junkies might even plan an entire series, one on each holiday.

Regardless of what you're mulling, here's a quartet of possibilities to give you a head start (you can play them super-straight or add your own zing):

- NEW YEAR'S EVE — Check out the nearby fireworks (or observe your dog going nuts as he/she/it listens to the thunderous booms). Avoid freeway alcoholics by hosting a party at home (steering tipsy buddies to your guest room to sleep it off). Fly to Manhattan to watch the Times Square ball drop, or stare into space from a friend's houseboat to see what you can see in the sky at midnight. Or travel to Christmas Island (aka Kiritimati), a Pacific Ocean atoll that's the first inhabited place on Earth to greet the incoming year because of its time zone.
- MOTHER'S DAY (Father's Day or Grandparents' Day) — Map out an event aimed strictly at satisfying

the known fancies of your target person. Organize a gourmet picnic or one with mystery-meat hot dogs. Climb a hill or meander through a forest with your partner (with mom or dad, nana or gramps huffin' and puffin' slightly behind).

- HALLOWEEN — Carve amusing or grotesque jack-o-lanterns and roast the pumpkin seeds, visit a local haunted house (one created just for the day or a mansion supposedly rife with ghosts), or risk censure by trick-or-treating despite being adults. Visit the creepy displays, big 'n' small, right in your own neighborhood.
- CHRISTMAS — Write your own naughty-and-nice lists and (at your own risk) do something related to some of their components. Create your own ornaments out of recycled materials (maybe even garbage), string cranberries or tinsel or something no one's ever strung before, go caroling at a senior facility or children's hospital (or both), tour a nearby 'hood that twinkles with freshly hung lights. Build a transgender Santa out of snow or mud or Nerf balls.

None of that your cup of eggnog? Well, if you fancy a true nonconformist observance, you might pick your MysteryDate from among these seven:

- Rubber Ducky Day (Jan. 13).
- International Condom Day (Feb. 14).
- Lumpy Rug Day (May 3).
- Bubba Day (June 2).
- Elephant Appreciation Day (Sept. 22).
- Knock-Knock Jokes Day (Oct. 31).
- National Whiner's Day (Dec. 26).

It was my daughter Jan Brown's birthday, a big one for her — you know, one that ends in a zero. Nancy and I were visiting her in Yonkers, N.Y., and my wife had arranged with a public library to open up an auditorium that seated a couple of hundred people so she could give a free concert and dedicate it to Jan. Library officials agreed and pledged to do publicity. They failed. Miserably. So, when six members of my family arrived, we found one couple that had wandered in. Nance gave the concert anyway.

Valentine's Day, of course, will forever be *the* day everyone waits for (or dreads because of impossibly high hopes). One way to celebrate it differently would be to participate in a holiday MysteryDate pillow fight.

In San Francisco, about 1,000 people usually descend on Justin Herman Plaza (on the edge of downtown) with feather-stuffed pillows and smack strangers until a sentinel whistles them to cease and desist. Other cities stage the event on non-holiday days. Either way, it's suggested you remove your eye- or sunglasses, anticipate covering your mouth with a bandana or mask so you don't choke on the plumes, and have some Tiger Balm or other muscle medicine handy to rub into sore arms afterwards.

Among similar skirmishes is a meet-up pillow-fight group programmed in London, Ontario — in the snow.

And in New York City, a group of concerned citizens called Pillows or Puppies have handed out trash bags to collect the feathery debris left behind. They've donated it *and* the deflated pillows they've picked up to local churches and homeless shelters.

I must confess: That idea tickles me.

Site unseen

My favorite special-day MysteryDate worked well except for its onset, when I led Nance to our car blindfolded. She didn't care for that part at all; it spurred an unexpected touch of claustrophobia despite her totally trusting I'd never hurt her or do anything menacing. Bottom line: She griped. But only for a short while.

I'd driven in big circles for nearly 20 minutes, even going the wrong way several times, so she'd lose all sense of direction. Eventually we arrived at the pizzeria where she had squealed "Woody, is that you in middle-aged makeup?" the day that we'd bumped into each other in California more than a quarter of a century after breaking up as teens on the East Coast.

Fighting off a gargantuan hankering to tear away the thick silk scarf that blocked her vision, she stepped inside, and her sense of smell immediately kicked in. "Pizza!" she exclaimed. The two-seat table that awaited us was the precise one we'd occupied at our long ago, destiny-loaded reunion.

This time, I'd gone there an hour before to set up, having gotten permission from the restaurant's manager, so in Nance's view was a pair of antique candlesticks that held hazel candles that matched her eye color. Our own robin's-egg-blue cloth napkins, perched on fancy-schmancy placemats, had replaced the eatery's paper lap-protectors. I'd also carefully placed our silver knives and forks in precise parallels, to keep my compulsive-obsessive gland from throbbing in panic at anything being out of sync. Finally, to embellish my nostalgia with an update to remember, I'd snuck in a crystal bud vase with two red roses.

Too swanky for a national pizza chain? Nope. "Wow, how sweet, how thoughtful!" crooned Nance, who couldn't seem to stop grinning — and to guarantee the thoughtfulness, I promised not to do the blindfold bit again.

Two at the zoo — for adults only

Yes, I readily admit that when we first started doing them, MysteryDates felt artificial. And yes, Valentine's Day — above all others — felt like a forced, let's-make-sure-we-have-a-good-time gig. But we later discovered that it's truly not that hard to make the holiday extraordinary.

Stimulation can come, for example, from a zoo sex tour with your sugar (sweetheart, baby, darling, honey, sweet pea, cutie-pie, lover, dumpling, monkey, pussycat, muffin, snookums, or any of the 9,583 other terms of endearment readily available for you to use). A handful of the tours are marvelously designed to be comic, but the vast majority of these annual zoological garden events that take place all over the United States are straightforward (and fascinating) scientific recitations.

Regardless of the category, those specialty treks will tell you how, where, and when a variety of critters physically mate (albeit not on command, and in all likelihood not while you're rubbernecking — so if you have truly prurient or deviant tendencies, *fuhgeddaboudit*).

And because of their sexual focus, most excursions limit observers to folks 21 and over.

Binder Park Zoo in Battle Creek, Michigan, has offered *Zoorotica* at $70 a couple, for example. Similar entertainment can be found at a Boise, Idaho, facility, where the tours are 100 percent natural, naturally. The brainstorm originally had sprung up in San Francisco, where pre-booked celebrants (about 80 strong) now are loaded into a tram to view animals grouped in terms of homosexuality, group sex, pedophilia, polygamy, and sex with inanimate objects.

The *San Francisco Chronicle* once quoted a female keeper-guide's description of rhino sex as always being violent. "It looks like two Jeeps having an argument," she said. Animals, she also declared, "do everything we do, but they do it a little differently. The only thing I couldn't find was cross-dressing."

And a guide once told my wife that the loudest sound heard in the zoo was the annual noise when a group of tortoises mated.

A date for all seasons

If you're unable, or unwilling, to use a pinpointed, single-moment event for a MysteryDate, you might try "a seasonal special" instead.

Experiment with, for instance, an ad-lib *summertime* picnic at a sandy beach close to home (or anywhere you or your partner may want to try out new shades). Or you could hop onto a toboggan in Regina, Saskatchewan, or near Angola, Indiana, for a fun-filled, snow-packed *wintry* date — or travel, for that matter, to Tangalooma Island, Australia, where the sleds are made from Masonite boards to help you zip down steep sand dunes at super-speeds.

In the *springtime*, you might catch opening day at a Major League Baseball stadium, a college (or high school) campus, or a Little League diamond — or find a field of wildflowers or smell the blossoming roses (and, perhaps, coffee) at a local botanical garden. And *Autumn* may organically lend itself to collecting multi-colored leaves that have descended from the trees or jumping into a pile of them you've just raked up. Or you could gather a group of friends to pick pumpkins or enjoy a spontaneously created hot apple cider or hot chocolate celebration. With donuts, of course.

As sure as kosher pigs won't eat bacon, summer, winter, spring or fall, MysteryDates might be calendar-generated tonics for y'all.

Part 4

Endless possibilities

It's Tuesday — Trivial Pursuit night with your partner. Like so many other Tuesdays. Three hours of predictability via the same-old, same-old.

It's a weekend evening — time to nurse a glass of fine wine or a beer, whimper about the latest glitches on your digital devices, and then catch the newest *Saturday Night Live* or a rerun of *Law & Order*. Like so many other nights you can't recall. Hours that could peak at humdrum.

Over the years, a relationship that started off as dazzling as a rainbow may have turned as gray as an elephant's hindquarters. But MysteryDates® can swiftly restore your colorful dreams and shatter your crown as couch-potato queen or king.

Merely thinking up something different can be stimulating. But meticulously (or even haphazardly) executing your plan and watching your mate slowly realize what's about to unfold, well, that should make trying worthwhile, right? The reality is that you needn't be half of a longstanding couple to do MysteryDates. A pairing of singles that starts on Zoosk or OurTime might suffice. So could a get-together with your best buddy (or an assemblage). You can be male or female or non-binary, just beyond your teens or ancient, straight or not.

Same-sex couples indeed have often been known to excel when the inimitable, the unparalleled, or the exceptional come into play. But the truth is, homosexual or heterosexual, if you've been significantly othered for just a month or so, you may not be able to plug a new zing into your relationship *instantaneously*.

Eventually, though, possibilities become endless.

Acquired a new interest or hobby? MysteryDate! Moved to a new place? MysteryDate! Reached a new stage of life? MysteryDate!

Road-testing a new companion? One more chance to test your ingenuity.

You could distract yourselves with something as unchallenging as an improvised meal at a neighborhood greasy-spoon, or as silly (or snarky) as a night of checking pop-up net ads so you can sneer at services and products you'll never use.

For some, a MysteryDate to a Mass at St. Patrick's Cathedral in Manhattan could be exceptionally rewarding, while others might opt to party hedonistically in a hideaway spa offering deep-release massage. The ultimate deciders? You and your druthers.

Hot-air balloons or air guitars?

MysteryDates also are borderless: They can take place half a block from home or a continent away. Want to stretch your boundaries even farther? Well, the sky can literally be the limit — as in hot-air ballooning or hang-gliding.

Nancy and I decades ago learned we needn't journey far to whip our zeal into action: We can become tourists in our own neighborhood, the next town, or somewhere uncharted (by us, at least) in the state.

MysteryDates work even when your inclinations linger at mundane: A teacher-friend informed his class about our inventions and soon after, he told me, one student "hauled his dirty clothes to the Laundromat and suggested his girlfriend meet him there. He surprised her with a burger lunch."

Or you could jointly train your new puppy, horse, or kangaroo. Alternatively, concoct an all-green date (or one that's completely *non*-PC). Or...

- Go on a daytime date for *only* two while your toddlers are in day care.
- Join a protest or counter-protest vigil.
- Explore a dormant volcano.
- Watch an elder with ultra-thick spectacles blow ultra-thin glass.
- Stand in line before the doors open on Black Friday in hope of scoring a new computer or hair dryer or set of golf clubs.

Instead, you might decide to:

- Get one-day jobs together (such as joining a focus group).
- Tour a fortune cookie factory.
- Visit a prison or jail.
- Dish up breakfast in bed on a day that has no particular significance.
- Go rock-climbing.
- Burn off fat by having acrobatic sex.
- Fill your fridge's vegetable/fruit bin by stocking up at a farmers' market.
- Test your skill, or lack of it, at an archery or shooting range.
- Revel at a synchronized airshow.

- Meditate together.
- Participate in a byzantine event somebody else arranged.
- Take a kickboxing or Pilates or Zumba class.
- Ride a tandem bike together.
- Spend an evening playing dueling air guitars (or air drums, air saxes, air anythings).

If you're male, it can be helpful to set up a date specifically intended to please *her*. Female? Switch the emphasis.

If your guy likes to flaunt his machismo, dates that might pleasure him include reading aloud passages from an Alex Cross thriller or a war-story anthology, lengthy back scratching or rub-down sessions, or viewing the mock mayhem of a championship wrestling match.

On the other just-as-stereotypical hand, if your favorite female likes to show off her delicateness, take her to a chick-flick, diet emporium, flower show, traditional English tearoom, or frilly-décor restaurant that serves only lettuce-leaf salads. Or a place that promotes warm 'n' fuzzy pink flannel jammies instead of sexy, silky, ebony nighties.

To fully satisfy both partners, you might obtain a rehearsal or backstage pass to experience a shared favorite — or schedule a MysteryDate in which each selects an activity for half the day.

You could also lean on ideas from friends who've borrowed the fundamental concept.

Events assembled by organizations likewise might ease your creation burden and fill your date calendar. In our county, for example, the Marin Moonshiners took three-mile, pre-Covid hiking excursions by flashlight each month on or near the full moon. Participants brought picnic dinners and a favorite beverage. A self-proclaimed "fun doctor" who wanted people to "drop the mouse and get out of the house" coordinated the treks.

Backyard or Booger Hollow?

I steadfastly believe that if you scratch the cosmic consciousness, it will ooze more ideas than you could use in three lifetimes. They can originate in your own mind or be lifted from the cerebral cortex of an acquaintance or business associate. Inspirations can be cloned from internet sites, broadcasts, books, or movies, and tailored to fit your personal idiosyncrasies.

At least 99.7 times out of 100, according to the Woody Weingarten Institute of Made-Up Statistics, MysteryDates won't depend on rhyme (though you *can* slip in Emily Dickinson if you're so predisposed) or reason (except wanting to have fun).

Our first ones generated tons of questions, unnecessary complexities. As time passed, we simplified. The upshot? Heightened intimacy — as well as happiness, hilarity, and hugs.

Are you a romantic? You might attempt something as carefree and childlike as lying in the grass together and playfully identifying animal shapes in clouds, or as complicated as a treasure hunt with hints that end with a loving gift (or a gift of love). It can take place where you live or in Booger Hollow, Arizona. Anywhere.

Homebodies could engage, for instance, in uncommon do-it-yourselves recycling projects — building a shelf out of used chopsticks, constructing a mirror frame from old DVDs, winding old yarn onto a ready-made wire skeleton as Nance and I did to create a playful sculpture.

A nearby town's ethnic street fair might tempt you to chow down on a Cambodian meal, stroll through a Guatemalan neighborhood, take a salsa lesson, or view a Day of the Dead parade.

World travelers, in contrast, might coordinate their trips to take in the notorious running of the bulls in Pamplona, Spain, or the running of mouths in any given legislative session in any of the world's capitals.

A visit to distant friends or kin is always another possibility. Nance once drove me on a MysteryDate to Sacramento, traveling hours from our home in San Anselmo, one traffic jam north of the Golden Gate Bridge, to hang out with a couple we hadn't seen for an eternity. There we were regaled by the male's childhood memories, including a tale about him accidentally sitting on his grandmother's lap in the dark as she sat on the toilet in the middle of the night because her Depression-mentality habit was to keep the lights off.

Need to stay close to home with the kids? Well, when was the last time you fought off mosquitoes from a sleeping bag in your backyard? On the other proverbial hand, a nearby campsite might supply the enchantment you need. Or, if you prefer something more visually alluring, a National Park could answer a question you haven't yet asked.

Tons of outdoor activities are specifically aimed, too, at the lesbian, gay, bisexual, transgender, and queer-plus community. Consider, for instance, the weeklong LGBTQ+ adults-only "Camp" Camp that's occurred in Maine since 1997. It features the usual sleep-away items: arts and athletic experiences, campfires, nature, stargazing, plus sundry evening social events. But the staff also oversees crocheting, croquet, jewelry-making, knitting, and yoga — as well as a costumed tea dance and a pajama party.

If relaxation is problematic, if the word "workaholic" best describes you or your mate (or both), and if you normally don't get away except on vacations, you might consider taking a break and heading for the O. Henry Pun-Off in Austin, a four-decade-old event in which contestants vie each May to be "punslingers."

Cheese-chasing

The U.S. map is speckled with activities that you can home in on wherever you want. As a for-instance...

- A pair of friends who've done it suggest that if you live within a crow's flight of any PBS television station, you should volunteer to answer phones for a pledge drive.
- If music's your drug of choice, visit Cleveland and traipse around the High School Rock Off, a seven-night extravaganza that pits more than 70 bands against each other each year.
- Like to watch four-footed creatures doing what they do? Almost every community has its share of animal-related events, ranging from those in which critters are personified to those where biped Homo sapiens drink too much and become another breed of cat.
- Rather watch outdoors activities indoors? In a suburban Detroit expo center in Novi, you can tackle the Ultimate Fishing Show.
- In Minnesota, you can stumble onto Barnesville's Potato Days, celebrated every August. Featured may be mashed potato wrestling and a Miss Tater Tot Pageant.
- Love to luxuriate in big crowds? You may opt, then, to bask in New York City's Feast of San Gennaro, a

yearly wonder that draws a million people to Little Italy, where the Patron Saint of Naples has been honored in the street festival since 1996. A cannoli-eating contest, celebratory Mass, and candlelit procession are highlighted.
- A tad more excitement may stem, however, from Bridge Day in Fayetteville, West Virginia, where 300 persons test gravity by jumping slightly under 900 feet into the New River Gorge.

Prefer to see something unconventional across the big pond? Competitors tumble and slide a lot in a Cheese-Rolling and Wake near Gloucester as they chase wheels of cheese downhill in an oddball British tradition that goes back hundreds of years. It's become so addictive that once, when the event was canceled, diehard rollers brought their own wheels and raced downward anyway.

Brave new whirls

Does your TV terminal have a hidden magnet that keeps drawing you in?

Well, you could consider an entire evening MysteryDate getting bleary-eyed from bingeing on a cable, streaming channel, or network TV marathon. And there's probably something you'd like On Demand, nominally expensive or free. You could also exercise together to a string of videos (starting off slow so you don't pull a hamstring), play games (such as Clue or dominos or Twister or Yahtzee, starting off slow so you don't get a brain freeze), or stage colorful paintball or water-gun fights (starting off slow so you don't end up engulfed in paint or H2O).

Cost-conscious family MysteryDates might also consist of:

- A car-washing party.
- An hour or two helping someone in a convalescent facility or hospital.
- A come-dressed-like-your-favorite-relative event.
- A visit to a doggie park, fat-farm, or spa.
- A blissful chunk of time on rented rollerblades (unless you wobble a lot).

Or you can, with one other family member or a huge group, do something you practically *never* do as a family (barbecue, eat Indian food, work out at the nearest gym or "Y," or gather in the park for a '60s-style "love in").

Simply go for it — *whatever* the "it" is.

Remember, though, the idea is that all those involved are expected to enjoy at least most of the activity (so don't plan to see an insect exhibit if your kid sister is squeamish, play in a casino if your mom is particularly sensitive to smoke, or visit an ice-cream factory if your dad is lactose-intolerant).

Need some fresh ideas? Well, here are a couple of handfuls in no particular order:

- Plan a Tom Sawyer-type painting party (fences, walls, ceilings).
- Conduct interviews with family members or do genealogy research.
- Pitch pennies (or nickels or dimes or quarters) or play penny-ante poker.
- Tour a docked luxury liner, freighter, airplane, chopper, or submarine.
- Build a birdhouse or doghouse as an animal-loving assemblage.

- Construct a snowman or scarecrow (then whirl for joy at your accomplishment).
- Catch butterflies or frogs or lizards and then release them.
- Go paddle-boating.
- Attend your local firemen's or policemen's pancake breakfast fund-raiser.
- Visit a cat or dog or horse show (or petting zoo).
- Dig for clams or scallops.
- Watch big jets take off at a big or small airport (or sea planes at some distant shoreline).
- Pick fruit on a farm or orchard by the basket or bushel or pound.
- Solve hard-copy or online puzzles together.
- Visit a rundown drive-in, if any still exist in or near your hometown, or go to a film night in the park.
- Have your caricatures or portraits done by a street artist.
- Revisit where you used to live.
- Slate a clean-out-our-computer-files day.
- Participate in a talent show.
- Preserve plums (or apples or lemons or pears or other fruit) from trees in your yard.
- Do origami.
- Draw pictures of each other (even if none of you draw well).
- Finger-paint as a group.
- Go sledding or tobogganing or bobsledding.
- Tour art galleries.
- Swim with the dolphins.

Enough? You probably can think of others, within three or four heartbeats, that better fit your own domestic dynasty.

Remember, MysteryDates don't depend on how big a community surrounds you either. They should be just as easy to pull off in teeny towns like Kentucky's Bowling Green, Michigan's Traverse City, or New York's Plattsburg as in metropolises like Albuquerque, Detroit, Louisville, or Phoenix.

The cliché is, "It's not the size that counts — it's what you do with it." Yes, I do know that the phrase was meant to apply to something else, but when it comes to MysteryDates, what *really* counts is how big your imagination is.

Part 5

Walks

If you're traveling, you're probably already somewhere novel and thereby more apt to opt for something that stretches your mind. But here are eight opportunities for MysteryDates® that you might not have previously contemplated:

- Find yourself in London town on a clear day when you can see forever (or, maybe even more exciting, on a foggy, foggy one)? You can meander the streets where The Ripper apparently learned that the bobbies didn't know Jack. And believe it or not, you can also choose from more than 300 repertory walks — morning, afternoon, and evening — including some special items like a Beatles Magical Mystery Tour.
- Many communities offer food-tasting tours (a buffet of ethnicities) as well as visits to eco-friendly sites.
- Maybe you'd prefer taking a big bite out of life via a vampire tour. They're available in different parts of New Orleans and, of course, Romania, where myths of the bloodsuckers began. Tangentially, a costumed Zombie Walk takes place each year in Irving, Texas, coinciding with its Texas Frightmare

Weekend.
- Dirty Girl Mud Runs — aimed more at fun than athleticism over a 5k, 14-obstacle course — have been held in Copper Mountain, Colorado; Fargo, North Dakota; Kalamazoo, Michigan; Killington, Vermont; Twin Cities, Minnesota; and about 60 other cities. Thousands have crawled through half a foot of mud to help raise money to fight breast cancer.
- Want to check out how the super-rich live? In New York City, customized walking tours of millionaires' homes and clubs won't cost you a fortune. Don't bring a sleeping bag, though.
- Want to see enormous religious towers, so-called "fairy chimneys" that are phallus-shaped? Try hiking in the Cappadocia region of Turkey.
- Fort Ancient in Ohio is a distinctive treat. There, forerunners of iPods (and even calendars) consist of an 18,000-foot network of earthen mounds Indians assembled nearly 2,000 years ago to help tell time. In the accompanying museum, you can beat on antique drums, dress in 18th century clothing, stew about Native American history, and sample venison stew.
- Do spectacular waterfalls and colorful grounds turn you on? Visit the village of Chamarel on the island Republic of Mauritius, where tourism officials have cordoned off seven colored layers of earth.

Hiking isn't limited to spots like Mauritius, of course. Some of the most exciting treks can be found in the United States — in Glacier, Grand Canyon, Yosemite, and Zion

National Parks, as well as along the Appalachian, Pacific Crest, and Continental Divide Trails.

According to an article in *The New York Times*, in fact, there are 8,565 state parks scattered across the country, "meaning a place to take a hike, fire up some s'mores, or simply recharge is often just around the corner."

Nancy, meanwhile, has taken me, as MysteryDates, not only on a couple of free neighborhood walks sponsored by the local historical society but on an excursion to the Presidio, a former U.S. Army base now part the Golden Gate Recreation Area. It's gorgeous — "combining natural beauty and historical significance," our guide told us as she recounted tales of Army brats "who cut school to hang around The Haight," for years the drug culture Mecca. The ex-military area is sort of all-inclusive. You get to see several George Lucas film facilities, hills, log cabins to rent for parties, new buildings and old, the ocean, and woods.

Nance gave it four wows; I gave it four salutes.

Flora the ghost

Nance and I met in the lobby of the Queen Anne, an upscale hotel in San Franciscco, with a group of strangers. The bearded, bespectacled guide sauntered in, dressed in a vintage top hat and cape, with a mysterious expression on his face. "Ready for some 'unearthly' fun?" he asked.

My wife is a grounded, pragmatic Virgo with seven planets in Earth signs. Or something like that. She likes terra firma. But she was ready. So was I — even if her MysteryDate® wouldn't have been my first choice. We'd gathered for an eerie moon-lit, ghost-hunting walk, forewarned by the tour leader on his website that we "might feel a fearful chill, or experience something unexpected...like seeing Flora, the city's most famous wandering ghost."

Some of the photos taken by previous guests purportedly show "orbs," supernatural entities obviously waiting around for their pictures to be snapped by cell phones or digital cameras. Anyway, for nearly three hours, the group heard our well-informed guide spin melodramatic tales about haunted buildings and the neighborhood's ghastly ghostly history. He paused, here and there, to demonstrate slight-of-hand magic (tough to see on a night tour but in keeping somehow for any phantasms that might materialize).

Our peerless leader had pre-warned us "some artifacts you'll touch are haunted." Nobody, however, felt any eerie entities. And no one was scared. But everybody was entertained, and bemused. Besides, we all now know everything we need to about the "Voodoo Queen of San Francisco," which arguably will never come up in regular day-to-day conversations.

Alas, our photos were orb-less. Flora must have had a previous date across town, or in another dimension. She never showed. Or maybe she was there but we just couldn't see her.

Steppin' out

In case you were worried about it, walking MysteryDates needn't be dependent on leaving our earthly plane — or even your hometown.

Here are half a dozen notions that open possibilities no matter where you reside:

- SNICKER WHILE YOU STROLL. In major U.S. cities at least, and many others, comedians who are also history buffs (and who might otherwise be

collecting unemployment checks) lead laugh-out-loud walking tours.
- CLIMB A STAIRWAY TO THE STARS. Some high-rise office buildings have great 360-degree views at the top, by sunlight or starlight. Many house restaurants there — and floors that rotate. A different, vertical walk might be a rock-climbing expedition on an arcade wall; a tougher one could be on a mountainside (just not Australia's 1,141-foot-high Uluru, aka Ayers Rock, where climbing was banned as of October 2019 to preserve the site's sacred significance to the local Aboriginal people).
- DETECTING MYSTERIES ON FOOT. Consider donning a mental Sherlock Holmes deerstalker cap, unlike the tangible ones that decorate the cover of this book, then exploring hidden nooks and crannies of your own community. Docent-conducted historical tours are also available in many small towns. In addition, by chatting with codgers and old gray mares, you can collect fascinating tidbits about the unique character and characters of the vicinity. And within an hour of your dwelling is, more than likely, a treasure trove just waiting for you to walk through and investigate (if no formal tours are scheduled, just borrow a library book and create a do-it-yourselfer).
- FROM SEA TO SHINING SEE. Take a leisurely stroll along the shores (and, maybe, sands) of your nearby ocean or lake. On beach jaunts, piña coladas are optional. Sea-shelling is another option. You might also create an impromptu "soup kitchen" for ducks at a nearby pond.

- DOIN' WHAT COMES NATURALLY. Walk in the outdoor footsteps of naturalists or discover the neatly sculptured flora in a community botanical garden or the indoor exhibits of an arboretum. Ever hunt for petroglyphs, fossils, or arrowheads? I can attest that it can be fun. You can also escape the traps and trappings of urban life by checking out trees and wildlife on the footpaths of your nearby state park, where trained rangers offer more current info than either Ken Burns or the History Channel. In contrast, you can stay put and explore your local park system — perhaps a romantic slow shuffle in a light drizzle.
- DOGGIE DO. Got a pooch? Take it to a place you've never been. If you don't have a dog, borrow a friend's or contact the local humane society to see if you can do a test-trek before fostering or adopting. You might also volunteer to be a dog-walker if you don't want one all the time.

Prefer something more exotic? Vacations are perfect times to experiment with scenarios available only in specific places. Such as these:

- JUNGLE JIM. Enjoy pretending you're a Hollywood-type adventurer and strolling right up to exotic animals? Zambia and Botswana walking safaris are ready to accommodate you.
- GETTING HIGH. In Sidney, Australia, you can walk across the Harbour Bridge or even climb its arches, day or night — with a guide, of course. Do I hear your knees knocking? Maybe you prefer to bridge from Asia to Europe? If so, head to Istanbul in October and run across the Bosphorus during the

Eurasia Marathon. Or take a ferry across, from one continent to another, with an audio or live guide.

Diversity and Betty Boop

No matter where you live, the starting point for untold walks is your own abode.

When I was growing up in Westchester County, N.Y., I'd often meander into almost-totally Italian and totally African American neighborhoods mere blocks from my home. Those treks became an open-air mini-education. But it was equally fascinating to explore the "mixed" neighborhoods nearby that replicated my own. And that's undoubtedly possible to do in many, many villages in the good ole USA.

Nance and I are lucky to live near the 40-plus hills of San Francisco, which can prove to be extraordinarily invigorating to experience. But the city's diverse districts are fascinating even when they don't require major pulmonary perseverance: Bayview-Hunters Point (African American), the Castro (LGBTQ+), Chinatown, Japantown, the Mission (Latino), and North Beach (Italian), and each provides colorful alleys, multi-colored murals. a plethora of people, specialty shops, and unique food. Easily accessible, too, are Angel Island, the Barbary Coast, Coit Tower, and the Golden Gate Bridge.

Guides can offer pinpointed expertise, of course, on tours incorporating the Beat Museum that *Time* magazine once called "a nice mix of eccentric jumble and obsessive inclusion," or adjacent strip joints like the Condor Club where Carol Doda flaunted her topless 44-inch chest. For aficionados of the bean, there's a coffeehouse culture Javawalk. Usually on tap as well are distinctive walks for families and children, for seniors and the disabled, not to mention a slew of charity treks and runs that benefit everything from AIDS and Alzheimer's to a Walk for the Hungry or a Walk to Cure Psoriasis.

Specialty events often accept visitors as participants. Consider, for instance, the Turkey Trail Trot, a Thanksgiving Day benefit for high school track-and-field teams highlighted by a brisk run in the park — before the parades, football games, and belly-stuffing (first the turkey's, then yours).

For many participants, San Francisco's unique Bay to Breakers race each May turns out to be, as a metaphor or a reality, a walk-in-the-park. Creative, gaudy, strange, and wild, the race spotlights world-class athletes in one of the world's largest (seven miles) and oldest (since 1912) foot races. It starts downtown, goes up and down the hills, and ends near the waters of the Pacific. It's an all-day thing. And in some cases, an all-day thong.

Let me elaborate.

Streets are jammed with participants and spectators. Most viewers are not there to watch the race: They want to gaze at the folks who trot or walk along — with or without body-paint in every possible color (though bright pink and green often seem to be favored), on and in every possible body part — wearing everything from their birthday suits to extraordinary decked-out costumes of Betty Boop, cheerleaders, Elvis, pink gorillas, and vaginas.

Part 6

Imperfectly perfect

You've planned the perfect MysteryDate® but your perfect partner's late — because her imperfect boss gave her excessive tasks and she couldn't dash off as hoped. So what?

Or one of you gets exceptionally queasy so you must stay in instead of going out. Or, somehow, you've double-booked events. Or it suddenly starts lightning or snowing so hard that driving's treacherous. Or even multiples of the above simultaneously. No worries.

At any given point, Murphy's apt to impose his law that if something can go wrong, it will. So, you need to stay flexible — and have Plans B, C, and, perchance, D ready.

Nancy and I've learned to roll with the punches, knowing MysteryDates can work out even when they're de-mystery-fied, and knowing that if all else fails, we most likely can turn it into a compelling anecdote (or, bringing joy to me, an imperfect pun).

Some activities, no matter how well plotted before life gets in the way, may result in a date we label "almost perfect" (almost a perfect synonym for "imperfectly perfect"). The usual cause for a crash-and-burn appraisal: Pilot error. One acquaintance of ours forgot — in a "junior moment" (because he's not old enough to have a "senior moment") — to *finish* planning a date. He simply never remembered what his original, brilliant intent was. We found out about it much later, when he informed us that we were supposed to have been included.

Not long ago my wife and I had each planned an event at precisely the same time. Fiercely wanting to retain her secret, she asked me to reveal what mine was. After I did, she decided to reschedule hers for several weeks later because I couldn't. The upshot? We enjoyed both.

A close friend, Nancy Thompson, planned a MysteryDate at her cozy nest in a small town just west of ours. Although her husband, Alan Babbitt, was in on it, Nance and I — the "datees" — knew nothing. Dinner and conversation were wondrous, as was spotting a rainbow when the downpour let up. So was the main point of the date — re-watching *The Little Prince*, which had been the spirited topic of several previous conversations. The glitch? Our friend, drained from an ultra-busy week, fell asleep only several minutes into the film.

"I can't help but feel that my first group MysteryDate was a rousing success!" she emailed us the next day. "I'm looking forward to staying awake next time."

Bending with the breeze

With MysteryDates, as with most of life, it's best to be like a palm tree, willing to dance whichever way the wind is blowing.

Dinner dates, as a prime example, may result in food or service bordering on the un-great (even places you've previously eaten in with previously yummy results). And, when traveling to an unfamiliar destination, you can find yourselves a mite lost (even when relying on a GPS).

Other possible bloopers during MysteryDates (yes, we *have* experienced them all):

- Arriving at the right location at the right time but a full week early.
- Forgetting the travel instructions that you so carefully wrote down but left on a table near your front door. Or not remembering the phone or house number of a critical contact — or the name of the person/guide you were supposed to meet.
- Watching Fourth of July fireworks or a solar eclipse though a fog bank.
- Having the wind whisk directions of where you're heading out of your hands and out of the car window into the distant darkness.
- Getting vertigo or growing nauseous in a bus or car on a winding mountain road on the way to or from who-knows-where.
- Arriving at where we're meant to be only to find the wedding's been postponed.

From lemons to lemonade

Even a string of missed dates shouldn't dampen spirits.

One hysterical week we missed three in a row — our grandchild, whom I was going to take to a science museum along with my wife, came down with a mysterious, unidentified ailment that confined her to bed; a performer contracted laryngitis and postponed his one-man-show at the last second; and a local commission's emergency session we felt we needed to attend put the kibosh on our presence at a comedy night.

In order to make lemonades out of you-know-whats, we scrambled and managed to substitute just as many new MysteryDates the following week.

As Nance once said to me, "There seems to be a lot of ying-ing and yang-ing in our lives."

Every now and then, through an unintended clue or slip of the tongue (often someone else's tongue), your partner will decipher what the mystery date's going to be. That shouldn't mess up your ensuing pleasure, though. Don't cancel. Rather, follow through with what you've so painstakingly arranged. Just as your sense of well-being may be enhanced by a chiropractor fine-tuning your spinal column, you adjusting to your partner knowing what's ahead might keep you from simulating Debby or Donny Downer.

Nance and I have also learned we should never give up prematurely. There was a particular musical I'd wanted to take her to, but the cost of tickets was well above my willingness to pay. Instead of resigning myself to *not* going, however, I checked and re-checked online sites that list twofers. Nada. For weeks. But guess what? Discounts for precisely what I wanted became available midway through the show's run, at almost 75 percent off, and we got to attend on a convenient night.

Patience may not always be its own reward, but cut-rate tickets assuredly can make me feel good.

Salvage what you can

Great Expectations is more than the title of a classic Charles Dickens novel: One particular MysteryDate that Nance pre-arranged early in our marriage was crammed with them.

The trouble was, she hadn't consulted a weatherwoman.

Understand that my wife loves to sail, a factoid that might have led to her blind spot. Nance had a friend in Boston with a boat. She'd been his frequent guest, learned how to pull in the sails, duck when they came about, help with the food, and wind rope. I've always preferred watching waves from the safety of shore, but my partner hadn't yet learned that when she programmed the date. Firmly believing I'd adore going under the Golden Gate and across the bay, she chartered a boat (and skipper) and picked me up at the ferry dock after my daily commute.

"That was the roughest ferry crossing I've had in about 13 years," I grumbled as I disembarked.

Ignoring the date having started, the wind refused to stop howling and growling. The waves rocked more than I'd ever had to cope with before. We both clutched our life jackets, hoping and praying that the storm would soon dissipate. Nance later told me *all* my skin color drained away.

We knew before it ended that the experience would be relegated to near-legendary status as the one that nearly washed away my desire to continue doing MysteryDates. It didn't, thank goodness — partially because my wife took me to my favorite restaurant afterward as an instant date "tack-on" to make up for the debacle. It allowed us to luxuriate in squab instead of squall.

That sail also became a huge red flag for what we now do before going anywhere: Be certain the date's most likely to please the other person and, if either of us is shaky at all, be ready to scrap the idea. Or at least have some motion-sickness pills handy.

And take any positive possible from the encounter.

Certainly, "almost-perfect" MysteryDates can detonate not only because of "too much" (as in water and wind), because of "not enough" (those unmet expectations), or because of being "out of our control" (when somebody else bungles things).

Unfulfilled hopes can be illustrated by the time Nance took me to a library to hear a guy she was sure would perform humorous ditties, Dr. Seuss parodies, and other light-hearted stuff. He didn't. We don't know where his head was that day, but he merely offered his original seriously redundant serious songs with seriously redundant lyrics.

Oops!

Concurrent mental currents

Nance had heard about it from a friend. An ideal MysteryDate, she thought. So, she scribbled the name of the place on a Post-it. I'd read about it in the daily newspaper. An ideal MysteryDate, I thought. So, I scribbled the name of the place on a Post-it.

But neither of us had yet set a specific day for the date when the "spoiler alert" happened. Her note slipped from her purse onto the floor, and she didn't see it where it landed, under our kitchen table. When I retrieved it and read it out of sheer curiosity (an occupational hazard for a lifelong journalist), I let her know I'd been planning to take her there.

We stared at each other for a moment, then chuckled in unison. And decided to go anyway — to the restaurant-club called AsiaSF, where transgender stars do double duty as performers and waitresses. Their stunning physical countenance is matched by the ambiance, the radiance of their attire, and their routines (not to mention the Cal-Asian food that's served)

We've been back repeatedly since, especially when we're hosting out-of-towners who aren't in on the imperfectly perfect "secret" of the eye-catching girls. We love watching our guests' awareness materialize. Inch by inch.

Part 7

Eating

MysteryDates® can revolve around a mega-expensive prix fixe dinner at a posh faraway palace or a chicken burrito at a fast-food emporium in the 'hood.

Eating events can involve any of countless restaurants within driving distance, munching on a calorie cornucopia while exiting a drive-in, picnicking on a moon-lit or sun-baked park bench or rooftop, or engaging in a gorge-athon at home.

You can spend hours staring at your partner's cheekbones past a dripping candle in a hidden, romantic corner of an upscale, Michelin-starred eatery. Or you can fix a snack or dessert for your mate, scarf up a takeout (or delivered) meal in bed, or have a surprise potluck in your dining room. You can binge at an inexpensive buffet on food that peaks at run-of-the-mill. You can even inhale a sandwich and fizzy water in the car — on the way to a time-dependent date — if you're crunched.

Nancy and I have done them all. As well as eating a Moroccan-style meal on floor cushions, dining in a Japanese restaurant omakase-style where the chef picks out what you eat, eating in a dim sum hole-in-the-wall where we got to choose from dozens of choices of Cantonese treats.

But beware: Even when you're completely tuned in to your partner's preferences, you can mess up the timing: "Damn, I was going to start a diet today," I blurted out a micro-second after Nance announced that we were going out "for a bulky meal, one of your favorites" in 25 minutes. But rather than risk disappointing her by voicing any *additional* resistance, I silently accompanied her to a local shopping center where a national pizzeria chain was promoting all-you-can-devour buffet lunches. "Eat with gusto," she directed me, "and don't worry about your girlish figure."

We both savored the never-ending selections and fresh salad, not to mention the tiny dessert pizza pieces covered with sugar and cinnamon. My diet? As I gleefully wiped the red tomato sauce from my white beard, I said, "I guess *tomorrow* is when I start dropping some weight."

Several tomorrows later, Nance re-fooled me by taking me back to the same place. That date, too, was happily successful — as she knew it would be (the instance she clipped the twofer coupon from our local paper).

Eight is enough

Here are eight ideas that might please your MysteryDate datee:

- A THREE-PEAT. Plan to have breakfast, lunch, and dinner in the same restaurant, not necessarily the same day — as three separate dates that your partner will never guess.
- ON-THE-STREET. Pushcarts may be almost as extinct as pterodactyls, but vendors (peddling crepes, fries, tamales) can still be found near

corners in larger cities. Try one, their food's usually delicious. Memory of one in Mexico City lollygags in my mind.
- HOME-COOKING. Instead of the mac-and-cheese favored by your grandchildren, why not create a luau? Or a clambake?
- A FORMAL AFFAIR. Concoct a black-tie meal and have it catered — at home. It'll probably work even better if you hire a server (a relative will do in a pinch).
- A BAR HUNT. Do this during "happy hour" to find the best appetizer in your community.
- VALUABLE VINO. Go on a tongue- and nose-pleasing wine-tasting tour (or, just to be different, a MysteryDate you invent that relies on the other senses — hearing, seeing, and touching).
- A PROGRESSIVE DINNER. Organize a meal that involves going to several restaurants in succession. Or put a new spin on the tried-and-true, old-fashioned concept: You and your partner stop at a second couple's for appetizers, then do a soup-tasting with another pair at their home, pause by a fourth duo's for salad, a fifth for entrees, a sixth for dessert, and a final one for cordials. All depending, of course, on your not running out of energy, time, or friends.
- LATE NITE. Visit a 24-hour supermarket, to nosh at or graze in, at 3:30 a.m.

Dining in the Dark

Intriguing eating spots exist in virtually every sprawling city, every tiny burg, and every location in between.

A short drive from Philadelphia, for instance, will take you to Trenton, New Jersey, with its population of more than 80,000 and a batch of restaurants. The state's capital and the site of a major Revolutionary War battle in 1776, Trenton offers a mix of foodstuffs from a rainbow of diversity. You could, in fact, pig out just from what's recommended on the "Hidden Trenton" website.

How 'bout starting with the tiny takeout-oriented Bamboo Grill, which stresses Jamaican dishes (such as goat soup or oxtails), or Gauterico Deli, a Guatemalan establishment pushing the notion that you get a "huge amount of food for next to no money" in a place admittedly "hard to find, even if you're looking for it." There's also Rozmaryn Restaurant & Bistro, a Polish place that features a goulash-potato pancake "Gypsy Special" and several kinds of perogi (ravioli), and NJ Weedman's Joint, which despite its name and a handful of inflation-busting $4.20 plates, inserts no marijuana or refined THC into its veggie or fish dishes.

The city underscores, by the way, the perception that the city contains only a handful of Starbucks.

In Chicago, as a variant, you can pick from settings that, like most other large cities, showcase food that's Afghanistani, American, Brazilian, Cuban, Ethiopian, Filipino, Mongolian, Tibetan, and Ukrainian. And that doesn't count the available bagels, barbecue, burgers, Cajun or Creole, cheesesteaks, chicken wings, chili, desserts, dim sum, doughnuts, fondue, frozen yogurt, gyros, ribs, salads, sandwiches, subs, sushi, and tapas.

Check out your town or one nearby. You'll undoubtedly find just-off-the-truck loads of mouth-watering goodies.

Speaking of that kind of vehicle, food trucks are becoming *de rigueur* in lots of bigger cities. Probably because of the array of dishes they offer.

For us, meanwhile, it's impossible to ignore the goodies offered by the San Francisco Bay Area. In the city alone, more than 3,400 eating sites are open at any given moment. And the range stretches from pretzels and Beyond burgers sold from street stands to $350 price-fixed meals (including tip but not wine or supplements) at the French Laundry, a heralded joint a bit north in Yountville.

We keep checking out new places. But we missed one that closed locally before we could try it, a place that served a sensual three-course dinner in total darkness. Opaque, which still has dining rooms in Santa Monica, San Diego, and New York. The original dine-in-the-dark concept had sprung up in Zurich (where patrons had been blindfolded) and spread to such other gourmet destination points as Berlin, London, Los Angeles, and Paris. As of this writing, those outlets still exist. Laughter, discretionary, has been a probable dinner companion due to the fumbling and multiple *faux pas* likely to ensue. But the best part? Nobody could notice if you talked with your mouth full, chewed with it wide open, or had anything dribble down your chin onto your jacket or blouse.

It's easy to turn a meal into something outside your comfort zone if you choose — dining nude with others, for example. The Füde Dinner Experience in New York City for $88 (after guests have been approved by the host, Ms. Charlie Ann Max, an artist and model), is "a liberating space that celebrates our most pure selves, through plant-based cooking, art, nudity, & self-love," according to its website. Füde meals, a March 2023 article in *The New*

York Times notes, "are not exclusively for women, but in order for men to attend, they need previous participants to vouch for them."

Miscellaneous munching

Unique dining may require you to travel a bit. To land-locked Montana, for example. To find the heralded tiki-themed Sip 'n Dip Lounge in Great Falls, where you can see a live mermaid, or at least a make-believe one in halter top and tail costume bottom, at the O'Haire Motor Inn. The mythological critter swims underwater in an indoor pool you can see through a window in the bar. Half a dozen other part-timers also wear mermaid outfits at the tourist attraction.

At the same time, a restaurant called The Marine Room in San Diego may also be a draw for MysteryDaters. It's so close to the La Jolla Bay shoreline, it can provide a view of high-tide waves crashing against windows at seaside tables. When the tide is out, diners watch the three s's — sailboats, surfers, and sunsets.

Trinity Place, in New York City, can be another fun dining experience. It's an eatery-bar where you must step through a 35-ton door into a former bank vault.

Nostalgia, in contrast, could be your main course.

A filling station a couple of towns away from us happened to share a driveway with a tiny, five-table delicatessen. It was like a visit to my old stomping grounds of New York City, with traditional chopped liver, corned beef, and shooting stars-high cholesterol. Both I and our ex-New Yawk pal that Nance brought along — because he also can't get enough of that stuff — cherished it.

How do I feed thee? Let me count the ways.

A friend of Nance's collected a flock of female and male artists, writers, and musicians and christened the group The Irregulars because it met on an erratic basis to talk, hang and, of course, eat. My wife, as might be expected, schlepped me to one enjoyable group session as a MysteryDate. And then did it again. And, in fact, a third time.

To be sure, each of us also lugs the other when traveling to the top spots for whatever the place is known (Philly Cheesesteak sandwiches in the City of Brotherly Love, for instance, or deep-dish pizza in The Windy City). But we additionally make sure to catch as many annual food festivals as possible (though we haven't yet caught up with these goodies): the Hope, Arkansas, watermelon celebration that includes seed-spitting contests; a Lenexa, Kansas, spinach do that highlights desserts made from the leaf (as well as green popcorn); and a Mitchell, Indiana, affair highlighting the likes of persimmon truffles.

Eating dates can be the easiest for adding other family members (including, I suppose, household pets if you designate them service animals).

Our most memorable food date ever? Probably one I planned as a tiny but integral part of a weekend getaway Nance had known about well in advance. We looked out a picture window of the Little River Inn in Mendocino at rocks and beach and the Pacific. I toasted our good life. After we ordered, I said, "Okay, now let's pretend this is our last meal. What would you have the server bring?"

Nance gasped.

When, several minutes later, she got over being nonplussed and into my MysteryDate game, she delighted in the French bread laced with melted brie and garlic (ignoring, for a change, the fat count). And she selected *that* appetizer, unsurprisingly, as her first pick. The rest of her final meal? Self-indulgence exemplified. Her mind had lit up like a pinball machine gone wild: Chocolate! Lobster! Filet mignon! Chicken! Butter! French fries! Butter! Organic veggies! Croissants! Butter! Chocolate! Chocolate! Chocolate!

We both grew blissful about our fantasy menus, delighted not only by our "what-if" possibilities but what we were consuming. I believe that whether you are a gourmet, gourmand, foodie, or McDonald's regular, just talking about the last meal can be fun (unless, I guess, if you're on Death Row in Texas).

Do you live to eat or eat to live, and does that matter at all? In the final analysis, it's evident that food and drink comprise a major brick in our culture's foundation. So, if you're a vegan, vegetarian, carnivore, or omnivore, why wait a minute longer? Get thee to an eatery — whether you're thinking Jack in the Box or out-of-the-box (like, maybe, opening that $1,000 bottle of vino on the top shelf of your wine cellar).

Cin cin! Lanpai! L'chaim! Salud! Skol! Prost!

Exhilaration (if not translation) awaits.

Part 8

For poorer or richer

Democrats and Republicans have long debated who's truly wealthy by today's standards, who's not. But no matter which party's running the country (or running it into the ground), the gap between rich and poor tends to keep widening. Many folks, including Nancy and me, just try to stay afloat somewhere above the middle point at any given moment.

Regardless of what level *your* financial situation is at, there's still plenty of room for astonishments. This chapter's about where and how to inject more surprises into your lives — whether counting singles is a big deal or whether you're one of those fat cats to whom the axiom "more bang for your buck" holds zero meaning.

Because my wife and I particularly enjoy "the hunt" and label ourselves cheapskates, we've each planned MysteryDates® to consignment and thrift shops, as well as to estate and yard sales, where we've discovered remarkable clothing, collectibles, jewelry, and scads of other items. Treasures. And we once reveled in buying something for 50 cents whose function we couldn't determine. Years later, we still have no idea what that oval object is, but it's made for a great conversation piece and some improvisational humor along the way: "Is it a hammer for pounding stale French bread into crumbs?" "No, it's a dinosaur egg poacher for very tall people."

With the tons of cheapos, coupons, and freebies available, all a wannabe MysteryDater normally needs is energy, the will to fantasize, and a chunk of time to research what's going on in his or her neck of the woods (or outside of it). Here are some potential jump-starters for anyone, like me, who still bizarrely smiles at retrieving somebody's lost penny from the soggy ground:

- To find a discount, check out kiddie, student, employee, and military markdowns, as well as reductions promoted by AAA and AARP; off-season specials (like paying cut-rate prices at attractions run by Disney or a slew of others); and online coupons and Valpaks sent via snail mail. Or test airlines providing companion-flies-free seats; two-for-one restaurant books; websites such as Goldstar, Groupon, and TheaterMania that often offer twofers; or the TKTS booth in Manhattan's Times Square. And if none of that's convenient, you still might be able to usher at a legit theater and see a show without cost.
- Museums and exhibit halls periodically list no-charge days.
- Free food is available almost all the time, but *always* on your birthday. To commemorate it, you can get a gratis $30 dinner at Benihana's "Chef's Table," a dessert at Olive Garden or Applebee's, or a scoop of ice cream at Baskin Robbins (although you should consider an unseen cost — future spam.) Tangentially, one day each spring, Ben & Jerry's gives away a million cones (to kids *and* adults). And most chains, as well as numerous local eateries,

offer complimentary "club" memberships that give special price breaks.

- Online freebies also can add a cornucopia of goodies to MysteryDates. A few keystrokes can bring hundreds of cost-free beauty products, household and office supplies, newspapers and magazines, novels, software, T-shirts, and other items of clothing, drinks, health- and feminine-care products, odds and ends for children and babies and pets, recipes, and samples of almost anything you can conjure. Just Google "free stuff" on Craigslist, Nextdoor, or similar sites. I've found "priceless" drinks online, a lecture on newts (isn't that what *everyone's* champing at the bit for?), and a way to win VIP tickets to an exotic-erotic ball. Also, no-cost banjo performances, dance and circus courses, ice-skating, monthly tours of the Antique Vibrator Museum, and a "Project Runway"-like competition. Plus countless dollars-off tickets for verifiably world-class events.
- Local libraries, which regularly sponsor book-giveaway days, will sometimes supply materials that can be transformed into a MysteryDate — such as loaning you a ukulele accompanied by a how-to book, or letting you borrow a machine that tumbles rocks into jewelry, or, well, a whole gamut of games and educational materials.
- For more shallow-pocket dates try a picnic in the park (there's no bill and nobody to tip), watch a string of YouTube videos at home together, go to a succession of happy-hour sites where appetizers are on the house, or (if you're feeling nervy) crash a fancy party or wedding reception by donning

swanky clothes.
- First-run movie houses, which commonly advertise bargain matinees, often spotlight price reductions on slow Mondays or Tuesdays. Or they'll give you lower-cost tickets if you do a multiple advance buy (at either the box office or through annual discount books). Second-run theaters are cheaper yet.
- Let's presume your wallet is thin rather than empty. How 'bout going on a low-budget spree — seeing how many useful items each of you can find at a dollar store (where the buck truly stops there, even if inflation's upped the charge to a buck and a quarter)? Or invite friends over for a leftover potluck dinner where each person raids his/her/their refrigerator and brings a couple of delights that haven't turned into Petrie dishes yet.

Rent or swap?

Still in a snit about your budget?

You can limit mega-costly MysteryDates to special occasions — a 10th wedding anniversary or a 30th birthday, for instance — and schedule no-special-event dates that consists of leisurely sunset strolls. Or you might watch a melodrama some other night at an inexpensive community theater instead of a touring Broadway extravaganza. Or attend a pay-what-you-can night. It's also possible to rent almost anything for a few dollars and build a creative date around it: mopeds or paddleboats, musical instruments, photo or video equipment, tools.

Members of the LGBTQ set, meanwhile, might opt to attend — or participate in — a cost-free Gay Pride parade or rally.

Ethnicity or heritage can play a role, too. You could select events predominantly African American, Asian, Italian, Jewish, Latino, Portuguese, Russian, or you-name-it if either of you fits a particular pigeonhole. Or, maybe better still, if neither does.

If you're exhausted seniors, you can always catch a matinee and early-bird dinner and be home and asleep by 8. Any-age bedmates might decide on a string of low-light evenings streaming romantic or screwball comedies from the 1940s or edgy laugh-inducers riddled with the F-word from *this* year. Or you could even create your own binge-athon out of vintage home movies or videos.

Another way to get something for nothing, in effect, is to engage in MysteryDate swapping. The range can be from spending time in vacation homes abroad to joining a website or club that will facilitate you trading your trash for somebody else's treasure (*they*, naturally, will think of the deal as swapping *their* junk for *your* finery). Items can include ancient reference books, apparel, artwork, equipment, games, seeds, sports, whatevers.

I've also heard of swap parties where couples bring clothes they don't want or can't use anymore (too big, too small, or just sick of wearing). Everyone gets to try on and walk out with a new wardrobe. The only cost is the time to slip into a bathroom or closet to slip into something "new."

Spending sprees

Rumor has it that the so-called 1 percent is not limited by geography: The real Richie Riches reside all over the world (sometimes in spots where no one else lives, or where *only* other wealthy people can be found, or in penthouses protected from the peasants who live "below"). Rumor also has it they do pretty much whatever they want whenever they want.

I wouldn't know.

What I do know is that my toys aren't the same. Or how easy a super-rich MysteryDate might be. I've never, for instance, put down a million-dollar bet on red in Monte Carlo. I've never purchased a mega-carat diamond thingamabob in Tiffany's or started a hostile takeover. Or bought a thoroughbred racehorse for kicks in Kentucky. Indeed, I've never bought out all the seats in a theater for friends.

And I'd never bought anything from the IfOnly website (before it was absorbed by MasterCard in 2019). That was a place where you could choose to pay through the proverbial nose for unique experiences in one of half a dozen cities. Like $300 a pop for instructions in drone flying. Or tacking on a fee that's more than 10 times the normal admission price to feed sharks at an aquarium. Or receive a minute-long video shout-out from rapper Snoop Dog for only $15,000.

Topping everything off, though, might have been an IfOnly hot air balloon expedition over the top of Mount Everest. Cost? A mere $5.2 million.

If truth be told, I *have* mimicked the deep-pocket crowd on a couple of ultra-rare occasions way above my pay-grade — when Nance and I splurged to visit Machu Picchu and when we took a photographic safari in Kenya. But I've never been able to dig into our pocket change to find $98,000 a year for "experiential travel" as some do, or spend $248,000 on a piece of jewelry, $147,000 on a new watch, or $404,000 for annual yacht rentals.

The most I truly know about Wealthy is that it's the name of a small town in Texas that originally was called

Poor but altered its moniker when it got a post office in 1894 (the community still exists but the postal facility closed 20 years later when the population had dropped from 90 to 25).

If, unlike me, you're able to pay no-never-mind to price tags, you're in a special category that opens all sorts of possibilities for MysteryDates. You could, for example, charter a ride for two to the International Space Station if you figure on spending, say, upwards of $55 million a person. Instead, you simply might fly to Paris in your own jet for a single special meal. Or chat with Jane Goodall and some of her chimpanzees at the site of her Tanzania studies. Or attend the opening night of La Scala's opera season in Milan. Or contribute enough to get a private tour of the Oval Office. Or obtain primo seating for the Olympics, the Tour de France, Wimbledon, or some other blue-ribbon event.

New York City is sufficiently all-embracing to supply endless date opportunities for either rich or poor. But since it's one of the world's more expensive spots to live and work in, it's clearly better suited to the well off. Want to stay in *the* primo spot there? Well, you can pay $75,000 a night to bed down at The Mark hotel.

Eating choices could include a $595 prix fixe meal at Masa, which has only 26 seats and no menu. The "bennie" is that tipping is not allowed.

You could, of course, "cheap-out" by picking from the $218 menu at Jean-Georges in the Trump Hotel Central Park — if you don't object to putting a couple more bucks in the pocket of the ex-President.

The super-rich, of course, tend to vacation (or go on an elongated MysteryDate, as the case may be) not where we in the hoi polloi are apt to run into them but in the chicest places of the Caribbean, the Mediterranean, and Europe (especially France), often in private clubs that have waiting lists of up to a decade. The Guards Polo Club in Windsor, which limits membership to 100, is one such, populated by billionaires, heads of state, rock stars, and royalty. If we must ask what the fee is to join, we all know, we certainly can't afford it. Privacy is primary. So is security. So are the toys: Members have access to miniature choppers, recording studios, submarines, super-yachts.

Let's not forget that should you happen to be wealthy *and* sophisticated, black-tie-and-tails opening nights at the symphony and/or ballet can become perfect dates — with the biggest expense being a spanking new designer tux or gown. Ready or not, Giorgio Armani, here we come.

But even the richest guys and gals in the world apparently have turned their backs on the globe's biggest-ticket frock, a bright red burgundy gown festooned with Swarovski crystals and 751 diamonds (including a pear-shaped one at the bodice center weighing 70 carats) that carries a reported price tag of $30 million. The gown, the "Nightingale of Kuala Lumpur" created by Malaysian designer Faizol Abdullah, supposedly is still being squirreled away somewhere. Because it's still for sale.

Yes, I readily admit that if you bought "The Nightingale" for a specific date, you might have a hell of a time keeping it a mystery.

Part 9

Sports, games

A sport, by definition, is a physical activity governed by rules or customs, with the action frequently being competitive. It can be participatory or a spectator scene. MysteryDates® can readily be pulled off when both partners play — or watch — the same goings-on.

Finding tickets to baseball, basketball, football, golf, hockey, soccer, stock car racing, tennis, or other major sports is normally a no-brainer — unless you want them for the likes of a Super Bowl, World Series, or World Cup. Another choice might be, for would-be participants, new and used equipment that's only a click and a credit card away on your computer.

Although most Americans are hooked on one or more of the frequently televised sports, you may decide other activities are more fascinating to explore: archery, bike riding, billiards and snooker, bobsledding, bungee jumping, catfish grabbing, croquet, curling, darts, dressage, fencing, frog-jumping, jai alai, kite-boarding, luge, marathon running, pickleball, ping pong, pumpkin carving, scuba diving or snorkeling, synchronized swimming, surfing, tent pitching, underwater hockey, ultimate Frisbee, unicycle hockey, and worm-charming Zorb ball (if you happen to find yourselves in New Zealand).

The levels, of course, include pro and amateur, semi-pro, college, and high school (or even preschool if you have a kid or grandkid of that age). Watching T-ball might be as entertaining for you as catching a multi-million-dollar Major League Baseball pro in action.

If you dislike crowds or being outdoors, you can stick to cable, network television, On Demand, or some other pay-TV or streaming choice. You can lose yourselves in fantasy (or real) betting.

Pseudo-sports events such as chess matches, poker tournaments, and trivia contests (in auditoriums, bars, or online at the Geeks Who Drink website) also are available for the asking.

Some MysteryDaters will lean toward yet another option — an array of home-based, sexually-based "indoor sports."

Want to wander, instead, way, way off the beaten track? In Utah, a Brian Head resort's fireworks and torchlight parade each Independence Day showcases more than 100 skiers and snowboarders heading down the mountain in formation. A pyrotechnic show follows. And Talatin, Oregon, has become — for at least a decade and a half now — the site of an annual fall West Coast Giant Pumpkin Regatta in which folks hollow out huge pumpkins (in the unbelievable vicinity of 1,000 pounds each) and paddle across a lake (sometimes dressed as tooth fairies or superheroes).

For a globe-trotting date, you could fly to the Middle East to watch a camel race. A highly popular sport in the United Arab Emirates (home of 14,000 active racing camels), it was originally staged at special festivals or weddings. But custom tracks now have been built to accommodate competitions from October to April. One of the best, which draws worldwide entrants, takes place each year at Al Wathba in Abu Dhabi.

Camels, known as "ships of the desert," are specially bred to compete (they can run up to 40 mph, though the normal pace is half that). Streamlined versions have teeny humps. Likewise teeny, until they became the center of an international controversy, were the six- and seven-year-old boy jockeys selected because they weighed so little and that would allow greater speed. The hullabaloo came about because many jockeys were recruited from foreign countries. Now, some fans shout "thank goodness" because jockeys below the age of 15 are banned.

In Australia, where camels are much slower than Arabians because of genetic and breeding differences, jockeys are mostly women.

Your pocketbook and inclinations will determine what you'll do about any of these items. If nothing else, though, playing or watching sports can provide you with hundreds of often used or mixed metaphors to be dropped into your conversations. Which, you might say, can be a slam-dunk.

Antidote to an allergy

For decades, Nancy was allergic to sports (chiefly boxing or hockey, which produce streams of blood, and football, where concussed players get carried off the field on gurneys with alarming frequency). I know that may seem strange since apparently the rest of the western world's permanently glued to news flashes about athletes and college basketball's bracketed March Madness — and attends contests of all sorts.

How'd she become turned off? At eight, her dad took her to her first baseball game, at Briggs Stadium in Detroit. As a diamond virgin, she says, she watched a bunch of old men in tight suits play catch over and over while chewing lots of alien substances, spitting with regularity, and frequently cupping their hands between their legs. She was not intrigued. To her, "the great American pastime" was a boring, incomprehensible waste of time.

She didn't realize, or care, that she was witnessing a rare no-hitter.

Because she presumed all sports were equally dull, her disgust expanded to all sports-related phenomena. Participation was never a real consideration. It became a standing joke with us that the sporting gods wanted vengeance. And got it. Whenever she'd turn on the radio or TV to get news updates, sports items invariably seemed to come first.

Therefore, when she picked up a pair of tickets and took me on a MysteryDate to the Giants home park, she knew I'd be surprised or maybe even shocked. The bigger revelation was that she appreciated the experience because contact between bat and ball became the sacrament of the day — highlighted by slugger Barry Bonds' three home runs (including one with the bases loaded) and a seesaw battle that went into extra innings. She also was entertained by a pre-game promotion featuring a cow aimlessly roaming around the field.

Since then, she still tends to recycle the sports section instantly — and still doesn't know the names of even the most popular players or, like the faux dimwit in the old Abbott and Costello comedy sketch, "Who's on First?" But she doesn't find baseball incomprehensible or boring anymore.

From wax lips to wii

Gamesmanship 101 offers something, as the cliché repeats repeatedly, for everyone.

You might plan a MysteryDate around batting cages, a driving range, or miniature golf. Then again, you could choose hopscotch or three-legged races. You can visit a casino or try to beat the odds at a dog track, jai alai, or a local contact sport. Maybe, however, you'd rather daub bingo cards at a neighboring church or veterans' hall or go on a mock treasure hunt (you can invent the maps and even the swag).

Always, it's likely, nearby arcades beckon (penny tokens typically cost a buck or more each now but may still translate, by today's standards, into cheap thrills). Happen to be traveling to Colorado? The indoor/outdoor Penny Arcade at Manitou Springs displays more than 400 vintage games and rides (and 20 different pinball machines). There, if an original game cost a penny, that's what you pay now; if it was 10 cents, you pay a dime. Etc., etc., and so forth, up to about $1.50.

Bowling alleys and poker parlors can also supply old-fashioned fun for MysteryDaters (your own living room might substitute nicely for that latter activity).

And with a pinch of ingenuity and perseverance, you can make up your own games. You might, for instance, create a YouTube night in which you and your partner watch whatever video games you randomly click on. You can also do a date in which you listen to the same music on two antique iPods while dancing or caressing. How about one in which you start writing or videotaping dual or side-by-side blogs or vlogs? You also might watch a reality-TV marathon of your own making or create a "long-distance"

MysteryDate by text-messaging while one of you is across town — or across the country.

You also might simply choose to listen to a sports-oriented podcast or three in the relaxed comfort of your bedroom.

Additionally, you can play word games or solve puzzles in bed together — or spend an evening on Craigslist clicking on items you didn't know you wanted. If you're into nostalgia, you might try recreating old-timey dances at home (anywhere from the Macarena to the Chicken or Charleston), maybe even in sports mascot regalia.

More? Try playing with out-of-fashion toys or games (Gumby, Magic 8-Ball, Ouija boards, Silly Putty, Slinky, Spin-Art, or yo-yos), work out together to a still relevant Jane Fonda or Jazzercise tape, or rent some ancient TV shows or movies (*Happy Days* or *The Ed Sullivan Show*, or Rocky and Bullwinkle or the *Rocky Horror Picture Show* — or *anything* starring Pee Wee Herman, who just died in 2023).

Maybe you'd like rummaging through storage areas for decades-neglected clothing to try on together (and perhaps later donate to the Salvation Army or some other charity). Such as bellbottoms, Bermuda shorts, a coonskin cap, go-go boots, hot pants or a miniskirt, a leisure suit or Nehru jacket, a poodle skirt or platform shoes, a raccoon coat or zoot suit saddle shoes, or a tie-dyed T-shirt.

It's possible, too, to don those duds and fold in a second part of the MysteryDate — such as going to a place like a retro club where you can disco or swing or jitterbug all decked out in garb of yesteryear. Or by inviting some friends in to dine on food from a bygone era, play retro music and dance at home (or outside it, even inviting the neighbors to join in so they don't call the cops).

Perhaps — instead of or in addition to — you'd want to scavenge-hunt your collective minds to compile a list of things that have disappeared except in the way-back of thrift stores. Not necessarily to buy but just to smile about. Contemplate for starters Atari and Pac-Man video games, beanbag chairs, Beanie babies, Big Boy carhop outfits, Bobby sox, cassette tapes, eight-tracks, Erector sets, green stamps, home-movie projectors, lava lamps, LPs, mimeograph machines, tiddlywinks, wax lips, and wooden nickels (aka slugs).

Hey, you're up!

Since so many activities, people, and places have vanished, a non-mental alternative might be to see if you can track down (even if you never experienced them when they were popular) a still-extant drive-in movie, a goldfish to swallow, a telephone booth to cram into, a set of TV rabbit ears to twist into or out of shape. How about searchig for old, short-term Christmas favorites like the Cabbage Patch Kids, Pet Rocks, the Tamagotchis, Tickle Me Elmos, or Zhu Zhu toy-pet hamsters? Or you might check out any number of social media to find classmates, enemies, lovers, old friends.

Would you rather play live-action games? In that case, you'd better start now lining up other people for your MysteryDates. You'll need them for standbys (charades or Twister, for instance), drinking games, or more recent party faves such as wii team-sport contests.

Like so many other of my suggestions, none of these items depend on your address. You can be in Los Angeles or Bell Buckle, Tennessee — or playing Parcheesi with one of the 7,000 residents of San Gimignano in Italy's Tuscany region, for that matter.

Or, if it's July and you're visiting East Dublin, Georgia, you might join the thousands attracted like sprinkles to ice cream cones to the annual Summer Redneck Games. In recent times, they've featured an armpit serenade, dumpster diving, horseshoes (using toilet seats), a hubcap hurl, and a watermelon seed-spitting contest — and, the plumbers' favorite, a butt-crack competition.

If, instead, you prefer turning hints of history into a personal sport, you could make a quest of finding metro landmarks (in Chicago, for instance, where you might have your mate join you in taking a photo at the Great Ape House in the Lincoln Park Zoo, sticking your toes into Lake Michigan, riding the Ferris wheel on Navy Pier, or eating a hot dog at Major League Baseball's Wrigley Field). In Boston, you two could photograph Paul Revere's grave, shake hands with a cop, or take a selfie on a trolley. In New York, you might choose to search for Alice in Wonderland in Central Park, shoot a picture of a pay phone, visit the 9/11 memorial, photograph three different gargoyles, or buy chocolates in Times Square.

You also could entertain your partner or any number of friends by fabricating something specifically geared to her, him, or them. Like, let's say, a scavenger hunt in the local candy store.

Or your own guest room closet or junk drawer.

Part 10

Quirky

Weird? Bizarre? Odd?
There's a chance you may dislike those words, much less the idea of a MysteryDate® that fits them. Nancy and I normally adore the eccentric, however. As well as the phrase one-of-a-kind, a not-as-rare-as-you-might-think handle. So, I advocate — primarily for those who have a cuddly place in their hearts for the quirky and idiosyncratic but also for anyone brave enough to at least *try* something new — checking these out, either as watchers or participants:

- In the town of Buñol, Spain, for a single hour on the final Wednesday each August, crowds enjoy La Tomatina, probably the globe's biggest food fight. Tons of over-ripe tomatoes are tossed by some 20,000 revelers. The event has inspired copy-cats in as diverse spots as Dongguan, China; Milwaukee; Karnataka, India; Reno; Sutamarchán, Colombia; and Twin Lakes, Colorado.
- Coffin-racing, a parade of hearses, and a frozen-salmon toss are all highlights of Frozen Dead Guys Days in the Colorado towns of Estes Park, Nederland, and Manitou. The annual festival started as a tribute to Bredo Morstoel, who's been kept on dry ice since

the 1990s in a do-it-yourself cryogenic shed set up by his grandson.

- A Brooklyn basement might be perfect for you if you want to stare at stand-up comics doing their routines in the buff. *The Naked Comedy Show* is a monthly showcase (two performances a night) that started toward the tail of '22. A 2023 piece about it in *The New York Times* headlined its story, "When Comics Face the Naked Truth."

- The Idiotarod was conceived in 1994 as a San Francisco takeoff on the historic Alaskan sled-dog race. The idea was that you and a handful of "idiot friends" could tie yourselves to shopping carts (optional costumes are in keeping with the pre-planned lunacy) and pull together toward the finish line. Race organizers at times led teams off track on purpose, and goaded spectators into bombarding racers with flour, eggs, and fish-heads. The originators dropped the event years back, but other communities (New York City, Ann Arbor, Cincinnati, and Toronto, for instance) liked it enough to borrow it.

- The Lions Beer Can Regatta in Darwin, Australia, blends a race dating to 1974 with engineering skills, sailing ability, and an overheated desire to build a boat out of empty beer and soft drink cans.

- The Bog Snorkeling Championships in Llanwrtyd Wells, Wales, pits swimmers against mud, 110 meters worth. Traditional strokes are banned but contestants seem happy to don goggles, snorkeling accessories, and wetsuits anyway. Australia and Ireland put on similar events.

- If you think what's good for the goose may also

be good for your partner, you might take a gander at the Mother Goose House in Hazard, Kentucky, which was built by artist George Stacy in 1935. With roof resembling the waterfowl (to scale) and car lights acting as its eyes (once upon a time, they blinked). Although tourists can't get in because people live in it, it's still drive-by eye candy for those who revel in such rarities. The Paper House, just north of Boston in Rockford, Massachusetts, is another off-the-beaten-path destination point for those who like curiosities. It's a wood-framed, wood-floored, wood-roofed structure, but the rest of it was constructed in 1922 using 100,000 pieces of varnished newspapers. Here, they *will* let you in — for a teeny fee: two bucks now, though it was originally set at 10 cents.

- Some people get off visiting places where famous folk are buried. But for those who want to step into sci-fi territory, they could try a free 30-minute Alcor Cryonics Tour in Scottsdale, Arizona, where so-called "corpsicles" are entombed in desert freeze-tanks awaiting medical advances that could resurrect and cure whatever killed them. Cost of the cryogenics is only $200,000 per body. Freezing pets is less than half that price.
- Totally in sync with your partner? Only if you answer affirmatively do I recommend you visit the Museum of Broken Relationships in Zagreb, Croatia. The facility — which showcases true tales of failed duos along with tokens symbolizing those relationships (think wedding albums, sex gadgets, whatchamacallits) — was opened in 2010 by a couple whose togetherness had disintegrated

shortly before. Some stories are hilarious, others painful. In case you don't want to travel as far as Zagreb, a domestic version of the museum opened in Los Angeles in 2016.

From Burning Man to beer-bathing

Finding matchless experiences or places is easy: Simply make the internet your perma-accomplice.

Day trips to unrivaled places can be magical or intriguing even if you must surrender most of your personal space to a crowd that's bigger than you'd normally like. One example is northern Nevada's annual Burning Man festival (which draws joyful hordes to the Black Rock Desert each year just prior to Labor Day).

It is usually an art, music, counterculture, partying blast, but it can also be a foot-deep mud challenge (as in 2023, when 73,000 participants, called Burners, had to shelter in place and be stranded for up to several days because of three months' worth of rain falling in 24 hours at the festival site).

Nance and I inadvertently attended Burning Man's solstice-celebrating predecessor at Baker Beach in San Francisco in the mid-'80s — a vastly tinier artistic incarnation of the 40-foot bonfire event. Our MysteryDate had been scheduled only as a casual walk on the sand, but when we stumbled onto the about-to-be blaze, we lingered — long enough, at least, to acquire a mild heat rash and a major anecdote. The "real thing," of course, now features nudity and revelry, absurd dress and behavior, visionary artwork and mutant vehicles (otherwise known as "art cars"), and music, music, music (domestic, foreign and otherworldly). Plus lots of drugs, pharmaceutical and illicit.

Festival-goers are ordinarily prepared for the extreme weather changes that are common, with dust-storms and thundershowers being the norm. Temperatures at night often go below freezing; during the day, 100-degree-plus temps are not unknown. So, it's recommended that participants bring everything needed to survive — food, layered clothing, shelter, tools, water. And earplugs.

If that outdoor ritual's too out-there for you, simply seek a level of uniqueness elsewhere. A few ideas:

- Watch a duel, which is still legal in Paraguay (and on stage in *Hamilton*).
- Bathe in barrel-shaped tubs filled with dark beer, a trendy restorative cure (it supposedly rejuvenates skin and nerves). If that's not accessible down the street from you, you'll be able to find it at spas and other health facilities in the Czech Republic.
- Catch young girls in the Islamic Republic of Mauritania stuffing their faces because husbands rate potential brides on a scale of how chunky they are. Once they're married, the obesity obsession continues: Appetite-enhancing drugs and wife-fattening farms are encouraged.
- Witness a British race that's been going on in West Sussex since 1973 — lawn-mower racing. For safety's sake, rules for the staggeringly inexpensive motor sport call for all blades to be removed.
- The world's largest collection of gnomes and pixies — more than 2,000 of them — is now housed at the Merry Harriers, a business at Woolfardisworthy, Bedeford, United Kingdom, a bedding plant/perennials business that contains polytunnels that cover more than 14,000 square feet.

Don't want to travel across a sea for an oddball MysteryDate?

Why not create your own, then, by sitting in court at a murder trial; trying on "new vintage" items, whatever that truly is, in a vintage shop; touring, on a dark and stormy night, a lighthouse (either in search of history or light); ogling delicately at a nudie camp or beach; or finding work as extras in a movie or TV film being shot around the corner.

Or, if you know where any eccentrics live, consider chatting with a local one.

Race me, handle me

The label Kinetic Grand Championship might initially strike you as somewhat lame but the Humboldt County, California, endeavor isn't — it's one of the most colorful, fun-filled, creative events ever devised.

Its website cites participating engine-less kinetic sculptures as "all-terrain human-powered art...animated with moving parts like blinking eyes, opening mouths, heads that move side to side and up and down." The three-day free-for-all entails a wacky 42-mile journey each Memorial Day weekend over dry land, dunes, and water. And teams consisting of pilots, pit crews, and "pee-ons." Originally called the Kinetic Sculpture Race, the event dates back half a century to a sculptor named Hobart Brown challenging Jack Mays, another artist, to a race/chase. Each fabricated a vehicle from mostly recycled material, designing, too, an embryo of a notion and tradition that have since spread to Oregon, Pennsylvania, and Washington — and even for a while in Poland and Australia.

During the water phase, most inventions float. A few don't. Nance and I watched a gigantic Paddle-Wheel Riverboat become mired in the muddy bottom and then, as if it were a slo-mo cartoon vessel, sink. Our most fond memory, however, is of a mechanism that held four women who hopped in and out of their gigantic shoe-on-wheels singing, in ultra-squeaky accord, tunes penned specifically for the event. But a geriatric marvel, a kinetic kidney bean, a Harley-Davidson Willie Nelson look-alike, and a loony locomotive also helped us in our perpetual pursuit of fun.

The event, FYI, is hands-on for creators, hands-off for spectators, unlike another offbeat MysteryDate we've found irresistible enough to repeat more than a few times — San Francisco's Exploratorium, which discourages looky-loos. Its axiom is the opposite of typical "don't touch" museum signage: "Handle me, please!" plead its exhibits. Virtually every step in the exhibits "of science, art and human perception" can be a cerebral/sensual trip.

All told, there's more than 330,000 square feet of space that houses 600 displays (plus films, lectures, special events, and workshops). With and without our granddaughter in tow, we've relished shows featuring bubbles (some bigger than a person, some within other bubbles), an exploration of composer John Cage's work, fleas, monks making mandalas, a mutant detector, performances by singers such as Laurie Anderson, and the science of skateboarding.

Oh, I almost forgot — the Exploratorium, which not long ago has been renovated and moved to the waterfront, also features a Tactile Dome you can crawl through, "an interactive excursion through total darkness, where your sense of touch becomes your only guide." It requires reservations. And no claustrophobia.

Not planning a visit to the city that natives never call Frisco? Well, the Maker Faire — also held in Pawtucket, Detroit, New York City, the United Kingdom's Newcastle, and a number of other places — is about the joy of discovery through hands-on, do-it-yourself technology and projects. They call it a "world's fair of hackers and tinkerers, a science fair for adults" (although children are also welcome).

The gamut is, uh, gamut-like: Exhibits are artistic, electronic, hand-cranked, interactive, pyrotechnic, robotic, and whimsical. Past hits have included a candy contraption that melts sugar with hot air, cupcakes on wheels, an electric giraffe, a lollipop-licking machine, a monorail for puppies, a musical synthesizer for six, paper airplanes, a radio-controlled submarine, a three-story Victorian house on wheels, a video-enabled rocket. And there have been unique live performances such as fountains made by dropping Mentos into bottles of Diet Coke.

If, in contrast, your flights of imagination carry you to other worlds, explore Flatwoods, West Virginia, where in 1952 an Unidentified Flying Object supposedly landed and released a hissing 7- to 10-foot-high, green armor-wearing, red-faced, bulging-eyed creature that purportedly spit out a poison gas. The only real hint of the saucer or its occupant today, though, is a sign in town that welcomes visitors to the "Home of the Green Monster."

Want a bogeyman of another kind? Visit the Ripley's Believe It or Not! museum on the boardwalk in Atlantic City, which showcases the skeleton of what it claims is the Jersey Devil, a 7-foot-tall, horse-headed, red-eyed reptile-bodied, bat-winged critter that haunts the deserted Pine Barrens. Oh yeah, the creature allegedly left hoof-prints over the years — along with bits and pieces of pooch carcasses. Repugnant maybe, but intriguing (at least for fans of horror or sci-fi movies).

Beds aren't only for sleeping

Most folks use beds for sleeping. Or sex. Some, however, prefer to use them for racing.

A now faddish phenom started in 1966 with four teams competing in Britain's Great Knaresborough Bed Race. The event's become so popular that the four have expanded ever so slightly — 120 teams now apply for 90 available slots.

How's it work? One team member rides atop the sheets (no standing allowed) while four pushing runners shove their bed toward the finish line. The use of helmets, kneepads, and elbow pads is vociferously encouraged.

The bed-racing concept quickly spread to Brunswick, Maine; Charleston, South Carolina; Farmington, Minnesota; Fort Wayne, Indiana (as part of the Three Rivers Festival); Key West (near the Atlantic Ocean); Louisville (as part of Kentucky Derby festivities); Newburyport (near Boston); San Francisco; Woodland and Morton, Washington; and York and Bedford, Pennsylvania.

And that doesn't count the Narcolepsy Bed Race in Roanoke, Virginia, or the Firecracker Run in East Moline, Illinois — a specialized hospital-bed race.

I'd describe it — and its resultant bedlam — in more detail but I stayed out too late last night on a different MysteryDate and am tired.

So, if you'll forgive me, I'm goin' to bed now.

Part 11

Adventure

Inventor Thomas Alva Edison's words were succinct: "If we all did the things we are capable of doing, we would literally astound ourselves." Adventurous MysteryDates®, I believe, can be immeasurably more electrifying than either Edison's light bulb or prose. They don't, however, need to be as exciting as holding a torch next to a propane tank; they simply need to be pleasurable.

Many folks might presume large cities would provide the best sites for my genus of dates. But smaller municipalities can be right up there. Consider Buxton, North Carolina. It's a quiet town of 1,400 known for its 208-foot-tall, candy cane-striped, black-and-white lighthouse constructed from 1.25 million bricks that weigh more than 5,000 tons. With a beam that can be seen for 20 miles. But that spot is also the jumping-off place for adventure surfing, as well as kiteboarding and ocean surf-fishing, at what's called The Point, along Cape Hatteras. The cape, once labeled the Graveyard of the Atlantic, is known for treacherous currents, shoals and storms, and a history riddled with shipwrecks.

If merely imagining yourself exploring a wreck isn't enough to stir you, you might instead choose to dive into

Minnesota's Lake Superior, where storms shoved giant vessels to the bottom during the 19th and early 20th centuries. Those Isle Royale National Park ghost ships are still pristine, partially because the water isn't riddled with salt, partially because park rules prohibit tourists from snatching pieces as souvenirs. The freshwater lake is a chilly 34-38 degrees, so the venture tends to be limited to expert or intermediate divers equipped with wetsuits and no fear of going down between 60 and 130 feet. Should you and your partner fit that criterion, you may never have a more breathtaking MysteryDate — even if you only end up probing the freighter Kamloops, which in 1927 ironically sank with a cargo of Life Savers.

Compare that with lots of spots in America's heartland that offer tamer watery escapades such as whitewater rafting (with or without a guide). It's easy. You put on a vest and helmet, cling to a paddle, then slide (and bump) down a river. Part of the delight, of course, is that there's apt to be more than a smidgeon of doubt upfront: Will you or the rocks end up dominating?

Those who'd rather have their fun sky-high and dry can try glider-tripping — with facilities and clubs that'll sign you up in virtually every state. The weightless up-and-down, sometimes upside down, silent flights chasing thermals without a motor might color your skin a pale green. Or not. Depends on how strong your stomach is and, I suspect, what you ate that morning. Novices can fly solo for 20 minutes searching for updrafts or select a longer ride. You also have the choice of flying together on a mile-high tow.

Not stimulating enough? Well, if you're a couple that perceives the hull of an airship as *excessive* protection, try hang-gliding. You might find yourselves peering at winged hawks circling below while you soar over bridges, mountaintops, the ocean, and a variety of villages.

Yet another alternative is paragliding, flying with air-filled parachutes strapped to your back. Yes, even greenhorns are being enrolled all over the United States.

Tons of other thrill-seekers substitute bungee jumping to obtain an instant buzz— you know, being attached to a giant rubber band and hopping off some precipice or metal bird into the great beyond. The aim is to bounce without hitting anything below. The sport flourishes all over the world. Cull through the possibilities: amphitheaters of limestone, cliff-sides, leaps into water, tropical forests. There are even spots where you can go in reverse, being shot into the air like a slingshot. But if you're truly courageous, just throw yourselves on 500-foot cords from a helicopter at 1,200 feet.

Two spanking new sports that combine performance art with danger have developed in recent years: extreme ironing and extreme cello. The former requires participants to take an ironing board to risky places and then press something. It's happened while parachuting, under the ice of a frozen lake, on top of large bronze statues, in the middle of a busy highway, and in a canoe. Cellists, meanwhile, have played on cathedral rooftops, on the summits of mountains, and during a marathon where the instruments were strapped to the players' backs except when they were playing.

Then again, has anyone ever told you to go jump off a bridge? One of the most publicized places to do just that exists in Los Angeles, where you can hike to the Bridge to Nowhere, then drop between the walls of a steep canyon toward rushing water that rages 10 stories below. You can put on a body harness and do a front or back dive, front or back flip, or combinations.

Adventure, not incidentally, is one more thing that depends on your own perspective. If you're a major couch potato, adventure might mean risking a cardiac arrest by popping over to your nearest shopping center to get a dozen donuts.

None of what I've listed above, of course, works for the faint of heart. Ergo, because many of my suggestions scare *us*, Nancy and I probably won't participate in them until some distant tomorrow — and then, probably, by watching. There's no fee for that. And no risk.

Speed or supernatural

Some pursuers of adrenalin rushes think almost everything is too mild to bother with except climbing a peak *without* the proper gear. I think they're wrong. Adventure can be in the eye, ear, and mind of the beholder. And here, to underscore *my* viewpoint, are nine MysteryDate options virtually anyone with a cheeky soul can perfect:

- OUT OR IN. Track a poisonous reptile in the wild, or enter a discount store the morning a huge sale is scheduled.
- CULINARY CHANCES. Eat at your in-laws, or find a restaurant that specializes in Cambodian, Albanian, or other exotic food you've never tried. Those who typically patronize fine-dining establishments might consider venturing into a fast-food emporium.
- SKATING ON THIN ICE. Participate in a roller derby or visit an ice rink when your significant other is oh, so much more skillful with blades. Skating on thin

ice, come to think of it, might also stem from simply disagreeing with your partner or adult children.
- CLASSY STUFF. Hire a boxing coach (who's happily willing to watch both men and women bleed) or take a class in animal husbandry and learn to handle rescued iguanas, mice, and their cousins at a humane society, SPCA, or wildlife rehab center.
- ROCK 'N' ROLL. Rock-climb, outdoors or within four walls. Moderately high or hazardously so. At the top, shout, "That's how I roll."
- UP YOUR HEART RATE. Take a lesson or two in high-speed or drag racing. Or try speedboarding, which twists skateboarding into an extreme sport.
- HIGH ON LIFE. Scaling a mountain could truly become a peak experience. Not far from us, in Yosemite National Park, is Half Dome, and halfway around the world, in the sub-range of the Himalayas in Nepal is Everest, the Earth's highest mount above sea level. We have zero intentions of climbing either — or Mauna Kea, a dormant volcano in Hawaii that is technically higher — although more than half of it is underwater in the Pacific Ocean — but *you* might relish it.
- IT'S THURSDAY AND WE'RE WHERE? Book a trip to Tibet or an even-less-traveled destination point through an agency that specializes in adventure travel. Or visit locales that have been abandoned by the tourist companies — like someplace along Route 66 — or sites most of those businesses have yet to find (such as the hill tunnel at Bateshwar, a village in India).
- TREKS WE'LL SKIP. Even though Nance and I aren't brave enough, you may have the *cojones*

for skywalking in the Alps (across loops without a floor) or on Canada's Mount Nimbus (on a flimsy span with slats far apart).

Skydiving — inside and out

Nance has done few things in her life that might authentically be categorized as fearless — although she did fly in a glider once, and owned a motorcycle for a year (selling it in what she called "a fit of sanity"). And I, who've been stuck with a lifelong inner-ear imbalance that sometimes makes over-the-counter Dramamine my drug of choice on vacation, am even less daredevil than she.

I often place anti-motion sickness bands on my wrists — pressure-point contrivances my wife's sure "will never become a fashion trend."

Regardless, she's never jumped out of a plane and has zero intentions of ever doing so. And, because she's plagued by claustrophobia, she didn't even venture with me into the tiny caves under churches in Peru or the catacombs of Italy when we toured. But many readers, I know, are sure that jeopardy itself is a kick worth pursuing and, therefore, can plan exploit after exploration without an instant of misgiving.

The height of adventure dating, Nance and I agree, would be side-by-side skydiving. We're too chicken to try it, though — believe it or don't — we do have acquaintances that have. *You* can book that activity with a multitude of companies and tumble in tandem or choose to do an accelerated freefall. Or work your way up to jumping in formation with other diving divas.

And if you get off on living on the edge, you can risk death with extreme-skydiving — that is, "flying" over rocky, snowy mountains at 110 mph and becoming a human glider before opening your parachute only a score of yards above the snow.

Another option? Jumping from more than 30,000 feet up (as some who seek to raise awareness about global warming do with regularity).

Does the question "What happens if the chute doesn't open?" still tug at the fringes of your brain? If your answer is yes, "indoor skydiving" is available. It's a faddish endeavor that, according to ads, "is safe for kids, challenging for adults, exciting for teens, and realistic for skydivers." Those same ads promote the vertical wind tunnel "for ages 3 to 93" by contending that "No experience is necessary." What *is* necessary to take a stab at "bodyflying" is training via an instructional video followed by a question-and-answer session — plus coaching on body position and hand signals. Add to that some flight gear (goggles, helmet and flying suit, knee and elbow padding) and hands-on personal assistance from an instructor who's within shouting distance at all times.

Entrepreneurs, of course, are happy to supply it all since you pay in advance.

Your freefall simulation gives you the distinct impression you're plummeting somewhere between 120 and 150 miles per hour. Yet there are no planes or chutes, and no real falling, jumping, or major elevations (you're only a few feet above the safety net in spite of it feeling otherwise). What happens is that you float on a cushion of air while utilizing the same body movements and aerobic maneuvers real skydivers use. But what you're actually buying is an exhilarating ride and spurts of adrenalin. Advanced flyers, who apparently get accustomed to the workout levels, can move on to back-flying, sit-flying, tricks and flips.

The first commercial version began in 1998 in Orlando. Others have since opened in Baltimore, Hollywood, Las Vegas, Montreal, Oklahoma City, Seattle, Britain, New Zealand, Russia, and Switzerland.

Want to overcome *your* fear of flying? This could be a benign way. *We're* still thinking about it.

Part 12

Travel, tourism

Spellbinding places to visit exist in virtually *every* U.S. community. New York City holds the title as top crowd-pleaser, however, by having some 46 million flock there each year to mix with 8.4 million residents.

NYC's choices are a quarter-inch short of infinite: You can eat in one of its 35,000 restaurants, check out any of 800 museums, and drink in one of nearly 4,000 bars. Or you can go to the theater (there are *only* 700 choices) or see a nightclub show (merely 400 of those).

But Nancy and I long ago learned we needn't journey across the country — or very far at all, in fact — to whip our zeal and MysteryDates® into action: We can become tourists in our own neighborhood or state.

My dad had taught me that lesson when I was growing up in a Manhattan suburb. He talked about how "New Yorkers miss a lot of exciting places to visit, places tourists *always* go to." To underscore his point, he took me into the dizzying torch of the Statue of Liberty, onto the splashy Staten Island ferry, and onto a crowded city sidewalk to see the Macy's Thanksgiving Day Parade from his shoulders — and he led countless joyous excursions to museums, parks, and riverfronts.

I likewise learned as a young adult that hopping a plane — or even climbing into a car — *can* lead to fantastic parties with friends or family waiting at the other end.

At the same time, I get to join millions of conventioneers and sightseers who are attracted each year to my nearby playground, San Francisco, where the Golden Gate Bridge, Pyramid building, and Salesforce Tower are all top architectural draws.

But none of those make many magazine lists of the nation's five most popular destination points. Those honors most often go to the two Disney Parks in central Florida and Anaheim, Faneuil Hall marketplace in Boston, the Las Vegas Strip, the National Mall in the District of Columbia, and Times Square in New York City. Who's to say a MysteryDate in or to any of those five spots can't still be a kick — especially for tour novices?

And not that far from the Big Apple is Beantown (aka Boston), where one can gleefully tour in a duck (a World War II-style amphibious-landing vehicle), narrated, logically, by a "con-duck-tor." Before splashing into the Charles River for a breathtaking view of the skylines, however, you get to cruise by the spots that make the area a birthplace of freedom and a city of firsts.

Also perfect for a MysteryDate are these other possibilities (also in alphabetical order of sorts, so I don't tick off the respective chambers of commerce while you tick off your personal choices): The Alamo in San Antonio; the battlefield at Gettysburg; Denali (formerly known as Mount McKinley) in Denali National Park & Preserve in Alaska; the Everglades in Florida; the French Quarter in New Orleans; the Gateway Arch in St. Louis; Glacier National Park in Montana; Hoover Dam in Boulder City; the Iowa State Law Library's ornate spiral staircase in

Des Moines; the Liberty Bell in Philadelphia, where my grandson, Zach Weingarten, is studying for a PhD while his wife, Krista Smith Weingarten, is working for Comcast; the NASA space center in Houston; the San Diego Zoo; ski resorts in Aspen; the Space Needle in Seattle; the site of the Valentine's Day Massacre in Chicago; and the World of Coca-Cola in Atlanta, where my son, Mark Weingarten, district-managed seven Mr. Smoothie stores.

MysteryDate enthusiasts need not be limited to famous places. Exploring locations without hordes of greeters and guides — a ghost town, for example — can become a tranquil jaunt.

Illinois has almost 50 such spots, mostly glimpses into long-faded yesteryear. For instance, only one abandoned house remains in Stachnikville, a fascinating coal-mining community that began life in 1856 and died 17 years later after being hit by poverty and sickness. Then there's Visnu Springs, which had been a popular resort town for Chicago gangsters in the early 1900s. A carousel ride used to please youngsters until the operator was caught in the gears and crushed. In the 1960s, the local hotel — now chained shut — was used as a hippie commune. The town's population vanished but the mythology is that the ghosts remain. And flesh-and-blood visitors still are welcome.

Maybe you want not only to do touristy things but stay in unusual locales. If so, you might go for TreeHouse Point, near Fall City, Washington, which offers sleeping arrangements on a 300-year-old, 160-foot-tall Sitka spruce (just *not* at the top). On the other side of the country, in Acme, Pennsylvania, the Tree Tops Restaurant offers twilight dining ($150 per person) or brunch ($9).

Prefer a lower site, a *lot* lower? Try sleeping in a 1,650-square-foot cavern in Farmington, New Mexico.

Kokopelli's Cave Bed & Breakfast is carved into the side of a sandstone cliff and is 70 feet underground. Views of the La Plata River 300 feet below are available, as are waterfall showers.

If those spots aren't special enough for you, consider Volcanoes National Park on the island of Hawaii, where you can see red lava that once measured as much as 2,000 degrees Fahrenheit.

Perhaps, instead, you'd just like to check out the location with the longest place name in the United States (and third longest in the world) — Lake Chargoggagoggmanchaugga-goggchaubunagungamaugg. The 45-letter moniker designates a freshwater site in Webster, Massachusetts, near the Connecticut border.

Across America, in major cities and in minor towns, car rallies also offer unique locales for MysteryDates. Teams normally are limited to a two-person crew (a driver and a navigator) who follow written instructions (sometimes designed to steer them off course) over a predetermined route. Clues can be as easy-to-read as "turn right at the library lion." Or as tough to make out as "take the left fork where the road runners run."

"Beep-beep."

Training wheels

My wife and I have twice so far put on our "MysteryDate training wheels" and ridden the rails.

I've long been a movie enthusiast, with eclectic tastes that range from Buster Keaton's silent comic nugget *The General* to the 2020's stunner *C'mon, C'mon* (which, despite being pretty much ignored by the public, made the favorites-list of another film buff, Barack Obama). But one of my all-time faves is *Citizen Kane*, the masterful Orson

Welles biopic that mirrors the life of newspaper magnate William Randolph Hearst. It's high on Nance's list, too.

Since I'd never visited Hearst Castle in San Simeon, where the real-life king of that roost crammed exquisite and garish antiques, art, and mementos into 165 rooms, my wife decided it was high time that I gaze at the plutocrat's peak of pretentiousness.

The castle sits halfway between San Francisco and Los Angeles, so she drove me to Emeryville to the closest Amtrak station, parked the car, and removed our suitcases from the trunk. It marked our first overnight MysteryDate, for which she'd tossed into a carry-on two jockey shorts, two pairs of socks, dark trousers, and a white shirt — and a toothbrush. She knows I travel light.

Nance had reserved a sleeping berth so we could nap on the scenic six-hour trip, rented a convertible and not-so-nearby motel room, and bought tickets in advance (all effortless on the internet). Once there, we bused up the hill to the castle and its 61 bathrooms and 41 fireplaces. It's amazingly decadent: extreme everything. "Enough" was never part of Hearst's lexicon. Acquisition apparently was his real middle name. The only thing missing was a sled named Rosebud.

Our first-ever train-ride MysteryDate, years before, consisted of a day trip I'd programmed with two friends for a Sunday in July. We traveled 75 miles south of San Francisco to the annual outdoor Gilroy Garlic Festival, where the heat whacked us, but the unique, all-encompassing aromas were intoxicating anyway. Joining 10,000 other garlic groupies and curiosity seekers, we taste-tested garlic fries (the best) as well as barbequed everything, garlic-flavored calamari, chicken, corn, pork, salmon, spring rolls, and a few tidbits of this 'n' that we weren't sure about. But when we hit the chocolate-garlic ice cream, all four of us almost in unison proclaimed it "yucky" and agreed the item would be an "only-once-in-a-lifetime, thank-God" experience.

Foreign but domestic

Travel can range from parading around the block to sampling any number of trips. It's assuredly *not* obligatory to tour the Mideast and pay somebody five bucks so they'll let you climb *off* a camel — or get *on* an elephant's back in Asia.

Have you taken a sightseeing bus in your hometown? When was the last time you went to a nearby seashore or boardwalk or desert? How often have you planned (as a MysteryDate or even a regular one) a day trip or weekender, or switched venues (city folks don't often go to the country; country folks rarely take the time to visit the city)? Have you recently rented a rowboat at a nearby lake, ridden a pony at a local zoo, or just checked out surrounding towns (maybe one after another after another, preferably within an hour of your house or apartment)?

Nance and I love, for example, to immerse ourselves in an ethnic bounty without having to show our passports. How? Well, we've gone to local areas populated with (or are gathering points for) people who don't look like we do. To San Francisco, where we've experienced Chinese (Chinatown), Hispanic/Latino (the Mission), Italian (the North Beach area), Japanese (Japantown), and Swedish (the Swedenborgian Church). To Berkeley, where we've mingled with groups of émigrés from India and, it seems, every other country in the world. And to nearby suburban Freemont, where we've found a cluster of Afghanis, handmade ravioli, and rugs, and some of the best Afghan food this side of Kabul. Because Afghanistan's cuisine has been influenced by China, India, Russia, and Persia, dishes feature the rich, sweet-and-tart tastes of cardamom, cilantro, rose water, and yogurt. Local shelves are stocked with apple tobacco, pomegranate juice, and sugared chickpeas.

If those places simply can't satisfy you, there are some 195 recognized nations in the world where you can holiday. Multiply by about a thousand or so, for the minimum potential places to stay in each one, and you'll immediately recognize that you could do MysteryDates forever and never repeat yourself.

Favorites of survivors of the travel-agent business are the Eiffel Tower in Paris; the Great Wall of China in Beijing; St. Peter's Basilica in Rome; the Sydney Opera House in Australia; the Taj Mahal in Agra, India; and Westminster Abbey in London.

Although neither Nance nor I are religious, at least in the organized sense, that doesn't mean we — or you — might not want to visit various houses of worship. A top choice can be La Sagrada Família in Barcelona, Spain, where the huge Roman Catholic cathedral is still under construction, a status it's been in for more than 100 years. But maybe you'd rather check out the gold glow of the Spanish Synagogue in Prague, a city in which my wife and I spent several hot and delightful days downing cold local brews. Islam enthusiasts might prefer the Shaikh Zayed Grand Mosque in Abu Dhabi, the United Arab Emirates capital.

Part of the fun of world travel, of course, is the variety of ways you get around — and the variety of minor annoyances you can overcome: bouncing in tuk-tuks in Bangkok (three-wheeled motorized carts, teeny and tight for 200-pounders like yours truly); mixing with chickens and other small farm animals in rattletrap trucks and taxies in Bali and Mexico; riding reckless rickshaws in China; and watching a lion urinate on the tire of our tour-guided open pop-top van on a photographic safari in Kenya.

But we've yet to attend the mid-summer World Bodypainting Festival in Pörtschach, Austria, which attracts artists from almost 50 countries and more than 30,000 gawkers each year. And we're unlikely ever to climb the treacherous stairs at Cambodia's Angkor Wat Temple, even with the ropes provided to help tourists scale the especially steep steps made to remind folks that heaven is tough to reach.

Getting there (anywhere) is a major part of the fun. Cruises, flights, tours — all, it's obvious, can be springboards for MysteryDates®.

My personal favorite mode of travel is air because it's the swiftest, most painless (despite the inevitable, irritating homeland security checkpoints), and, often, the cheapest (even if I'm still more than a little afraid of non-mask wearers giving me Covid because my immune system has been compromised).

The simple truth is, I sometimes get restless and just "wanna go." Somewhere interesting. Somewhere exhilarating. *Anywhere.*

But remember, no matter where a MysteryDate takes place, there's only one requisite: A willingness to try something novel.

If you own your own Lear, you can consider soaring over the pond to London for a spot of tea or a pint of the local brew. If you can't finance that, however, you could spend an evening on an *imaginary* MysteryDate with your partner (you do the research first, then both of you fantasize, for instance, about chartering a plane and trekking to a clandestine Peruvian palace in the Amazon jungle). Or maybe you can flesh out your daydream by voyaging into space on the USS Enterprise (with or without William Shatner, Chris Pine, or Paul Wesley).

Your mind's eye may be all the starship fuel you'll ever need.

Part 13

Spontaneity

Nancy and I are planning freaks. We both enjoy doing research, getting info, making advance arrangements. So, spontaneity normally doesn't occupy a massive part of our vocabulary. I've nevertheless been able to formulate an archetype for last-minute MysteryDates®.

My initial brainstorm occurred while I was pondering what leftovers hadn't changed color yet in the recesses of our fridge. I whispered to my wife, "MysteryDate — *now*," and we instantly headed for a bite at an un-fancy sandwich shop (followed by a movie we'd both been aching to see). It didn't take long before I'd become The Compleat MysteryDate Whisperer concocting a whole series of spur-of-the-moment events.

Now, if we're finishing lunch and either she or I decide on a blink-of-an-eye date, we might go shopping, meet friends, take a trolley ride, or walk somewhere-or-other. Or, if we're out doing errands together and one mate decides on an instant date, we may end up repeating an activity we long ago deemed irresistible.

You get the idea — the epitome of free-form, a way to keep the relationship fresh, honed, and spicy, and decidedly in the here-and-now.

Want a specific? On a steamy mid-summer's day in 2017, I read in the local morning newspaper about a "soft launch" for the bullet passenger train that was going to run between my adopted home county, Marin, and the one on its northern border, Sonoma. Free preview rides were being offered *later that day*. I jumped at the chance for an immediate date mainly because the train was air-conditioned, and our home wasn't. I also relished the idea of bringing along Hannah Schifrin, our then 10-year-old granddaughter who was staying with us for the weekend and who, despite having flown out of the country (to Mexico) multiple times, had never been on a train.

The halfway, half-hour ride was noise-free and completely un-bumpy, a major contrast to many commuter train compartments I'd ridden as a suburban kid into New York City. The California countryside was pleasantly picturesque. And the Baskin-Robbins ice cream cups and cones we had in a northern city before returning home made the day blissful for all three of us.

Nothingness and togetherness

Impulsive MysteryDates can take unlimited forms. Whims can be intricate (you might improvise something based on your age or height or weight) or unfussy (an extraordinary "mystery dessert date" or "mystery liqueur date" that follows a routine home-cooked meal).

You can in a flash invent or re-invent your own date, or pick, if you find a nugget here, from the following four choices:

- Write a bunch of instantly doable dates on tiny slips of paper, dump them into a hat (or cereal bowl, or your favorite vase), then follow through on whatever your partner picks — without him or her

looking — for the evening (or morning, noontime, or weekend). A week later, you might want to try another.
- Shout out MysteryDate and then say, as I did once, "The date's right now. We're going to re-organize our pantry and then, if we have the energy and time, we'll clean out the refrigerator and freezer. We've been postponing those tasks for weeks."
- Just while away the time on a "do-nothing MysteryDate" by luxuriating in totally mindless, self-indulgent, relaxing pastimes (couch-potato pursuits such as reading two trashy novels side-by-side or jointly watching *The Simpsons* or *Sponge Bob* animation on TV).
- Spend a "plan-nothing-but-do-everything MysteryDate" that lets you shift — together — from one spontaneous activity to the next, confined only by what either of you opts to do.

Being blindfolded, part deux

Need another real-life instance of necessity being the mommy of invention?

Nance and I were multi-tasking at home on probably half a dozen simultaneous projects one afternoon when an overloaded me said, seemingly out of nowhere, "We're going on a mystery date in seven minutes." "Can I wear my sweats?" asked my wife, not wanting to change. I inspected her — slowly and melodramatically (because I enjoy doing both the ogling and the playacting) — and then told her that because we live a casual lifestyle, she needn't give it a second thought.

What did make her think twice, though, was that I asked her to wear a blindfold.

I'd used the ploy once before and, when she'd made it clear she didn't care for it, I'd vowed I wouldn't do it again. So, she again became irritated and told me so in no uncertain terms. I pleaded: "Please bear with me. I promise that this is a special case. And it'll be a fairly short drive. If you'd rather just close your eyes tight, go right ahead." So, she took Option 2.

I helped her out of the car. We walked up three steps and I said, "You can look now." We were at her daughter's home.

That MysteryDate — linking Nance, me, and our then infant granddaughter — was one of the most satisfying ever, since there weren't any places that my partner would rather have been at the time.

Nance's daughter, by the way, had called me only seconds before my seven-minute pronouncement and pleaded for extra babysitting help.

The best part of the whole affair was that my wife forgave me, again, for temporarily making her sightless.

Spontaneous consumption

Like water finding its own level, every household tends to designate its chief shopper, chopper, and chef (as well as who does KP duty). In ours, generally, my wife's the planner and preparer; I'm the one-man clean-up crew.

But there are plenty of times she simply doesn't feel like even thinking about the menu, shopping, organizing the food, setting the table, or even digging in the freezer. She just wants to eat. That's when she has some whine with her supper: "I wanna go out!" The God's-honest truth is, whenever she rattles that verbal saber, her words tend to prod me into creating a mystery dinner date on the spot.

That way she not only doesn't have to bake, boil, fry, or roast, she doesn't have to stew about it for a second.

One time, she turned the tables though. "What's your favorite place to eat lunch?" she asked. And when I told her, she countered with, "That's it, that's the MysteryDate!"

The burgers were delicious (I ordered "natural" beef; she, naturally, chose meatless). Both of us declared the onion rings scrumptious. But the best part of the date was that it gave us both a break from working at home.

That actually twisted and fine-tuned my prototypical "you pick the restaurant" idea in one swell foop. A couple of years before, I'd directed her to take the ferry into San Francisco. I met the boat and said, "This city has more than 4,000 restaurants. You get to pick the one where we'll have dinner." Or words to that effect. She'd been dumbfounded. Some alien being obviously had taken control of my body, mind, and spirit since I'm typically a methodical, meticulous planner-researcher-investigator who confirms and reconfirms reservations after having quadruple-checked my datebook and hers for time and place. When it comes to food, elasticity isn't a standard-issue part of my diet.

Occasionally, though, when meals don't come off quite the way we've intended, I feel forced to bend.

We'd set up a regular dinner party, two months earlier, at our place. Two hours before it was to begin, after Nance had already bought fresh everything, sliced the salad, and diced the entrée (mango chicken) in preparation for cooking it, one invitee called and urged us to call it off. Why? She'd heard a radio bulletin that an accident would keep several of our dinner guests' normal route, the 4.46-mile-long Bay Bridge connecting Marin County to the East Bay, shut down for "an indefinite time." And traffic nearing the Golden Gate Bridge, the best alternate, was taking 2-1/2 hours.

So, cancel we did, finding a near-future date that would be convenient for all of us for a do-over. But a few minutes later I urged my wife to get ready for a MysteryDate. She found out shortly that I'd called a neighbor couple, told them what had occurred, and invited them to chow down at our place on an already-prepared Greek salad and store-bought hors d'oeuvres. The poultry wasn't on the revised menu because it hadn't yet been put in the oven.

After an abbreviated dinner, we all took in a flick on our side of the bridges that we'd been hoping to see but hadn't been able to squeeze in. Voila! A cancellation had been transformed into a soupçon I subtitled "The caterpillar becomes a butterfly."

Permission not needed

There are approximately four zillion, three hundred thousand hair-trigger MysteryDates you can actualize without thinking too hard — or getting permission.

An entry-level art or home-improvement project, for example, might work even when your imagination or your partner's is severely straight-jacketed.

Or you could:
- Arbitrarily alphabetize some list just for the heck of it.
- Assemble that emergency kit you've been meaning to get around to forever.
- Check your local newspaper's community calendar for something going on *right now*.

- Compile an imaginary or imaginative bucket list (or use a real bucket, hot water, and soap to scrub your bathroom floor).
- Craft distorted three-dimensional papier-mâché self-portraits.
- Create your own code (digital or spy) or language.
- Delete the hundreds of emails in your inbox that you've been meaning to.
- Dine with a homeless guest or two at a fast-food joint.
- Do a thousand-piece jigsaw puzzle or build your own Sudoku.
- Explore your ancestors and/or your partner's online.
- Fashion puppets out of socks and put on a show for each other about your childhoods.
- Figure out the perfect mental murders of those people you'd like see disappear (personal or political foes or just people you've never forgiven for real or imagined hurts or misdeeds). Extra points for never-tried-before methods.
- Dumpster dive (just be sure there's a nearby hot shower handy).
- Get some scrap paper and create origami critters that no one's seen before (or build mock Fokkers).
- Give in to your inner children and build a fort out of the excess throw pillows you have lying around on beds and couches and overstuffed chairs or squashed into closets.
- Listen to a podcast about how to deal with a new government crisis.
- Purposefully get lost.

- Pack a carton of goodies for your local food bank.
- Participate in a hot local pick-up game on your local high school or college basketball court (or, if you're still single, pick up somebody at a local bar to play in your own courtyard).
- Pretend you're kids again and write to Santa asking for some special technology gifts.
- Put together a time capsule for the two of you to open in five years or 10, or never.
- Watch cute-animal YouTube videos with a grandkid.
- Select one item each from your bucket lists and do them.
- Start a How-I-Can-Avoid-Boredom list.
- Write a letter to a vet in a war zone.
- Taste every free sample at a farmer's market.
- Turn on your sprinklers and run through the waters (bathing suits required unless you have a tall, tall privacy fence).
- Update your resumes even if neither of you are currently in the job market.
- Wash your dirty fingerprints off your car sides (or windows riddled with dead insects who had no GPS).
- Make a list of all the things you can postpone doing.

Or, if you have too much time on your hands, take the first of 365 consecutive daily photos of your pet.

Part 14

Museums

Nancy and I cherish museums. Of all kinds. So, whenever we travel to a new neighborhood, town, or country, we check them out.

Sometimes they're dusty, musty, and poorly lighted. Sometimes they're interactive and avant-garde. Sometimes they're artsy and unfathomable. We rarely absorb everything we've observed but while onsite we're entertained (frequently), educated (usually), and find our imaginations stretched (almost always).

Museums offer shows, activities, music, classes, lectures, multi-media, and other options (focusing on art, science, history, and, in fact, almost — with apologies to *Ecclesiastes* where it apparently was said first — everything under the sun, including exhibits about rays from the sun itself).

Sure, you can visit the Louvre or the Hermitage or the Prado, which we have, but maybe you'd rather see some place less traveled. If you're a chocoholic, for example, you might tour Belgium, where you can select from four dedicated facilities: the Museum Temple of Chocolate Cote D'or in Halle, the Chocolate Museum Jacques in Eupen, Choco-Story in Bruges, and the Museum of Cocoa and Chocolate in Brussels. Each showcases its own brand of cacao, the "food of the gods," and each provides a sampling area.

Have a fixation with gangsters — or crime-busters? The Mob Museum (more formally called the National Museum of Organized Crime and Law Enforcement) appropriately opened in Las Vegas in 2012 on the 82nd anniversary of the Valentine's Day Massacre. Get inside info about Al Capone, Bugsy Siegel, John Gotti, Eliot Ness, and, naturally, J. Edgar Hoover.

In that same city, you also can visit the Neon Museum and its "boneyard" outside, where some of its 200 old Vegas signs date back to when black entertainers could perform on The Strip but not stay at its hotels where they worked — a vexing situation that mercifully doesn't exist anymore.

Speaking of African Americans, a $540 million Smithsonian on the National Mall in Washington, D.C. looks at the race's culture and history. Coverage ranges from slave trade and Harriet Tubman to today's ongoing struggles for the vote and other civil rights — with stops along the way for a railway car with segregated seats for blacks and whites, a Tuskegee airman's biplane, Louis Armstrong's trumpet, the boxing gear of Mohammad Ali, and a fedora worn by Michael Jackson, the disturbed pop star who desperately tried to bleach himself white.

D.C. also offers an expanded International Spy Museum, $162 million worth, which zeroes in on both fictional and real practitioners of espionage, warrantless eavesdropping, and intelligence mishaps. You can also find in the permanent collection G-men toys, fountain pen and pigeon cameras (the latter an early, more natural form of drone), a disguise kit, a flashlight gun, and an original 1777 letter from George Washington, the nation's first spymaster, authorizing a one-time $500 payment to a Nathaniel Sackett to set up, as his "intelligence director," an espionage network.

Also, there is an actual waterboard, which *The New York Times* described as "the notorious torture used in the Inquisition, by the Pol Pot regime in Cambodia, and by the CIA against Al Qaeda suspects in 2002 and 2003."

Not your cup of poison tea? Perhaps you'd prefer the Museum of Bad Art as a stimulant. The often-whimsical Somerville, Massachusetts, space — underscored by sarcastic descriptions on each of the 25 pieces displayed at any given time (out of more than 700 in its collection) — is housed in the basement of a 1912 vaudeville theater that now screens movies. A caveat: The museum's open only when films are scheduled. Its website displays items under rubric-puns like "Poor Traits" and "In the Nood." Highlights include a pointillism-impressionist "Sunday on the Pot with George" and a tempera-and-acrylic impression of "Bone-Juggling Dog in Hula Skirt." Visitors comment in a guest book. One notes that a particular image's "nipples follow you around the room."

Find yourself near Pasadena, California, meanwhile, and you can treat yourself to a day at the Bunny Museum, which houses more than 26,000 rabbit-related items.

Clearly, when you think about museums, the only limit should be your own curiosity and taste.

Nance, in fact, once aimed a MysteryDate® at one of my longtime addictions, a legacy of my many youthful days spent in bowling alleys. She and a pair of friends who were in on it drove me across the bay to a Pinball Museum, where I blissfully played both new and antique ones for hours.

And only tilted twice.

Living art

Talk about sensual.

Walk into the de Young Museum in San Francisco's Golden Gate Park and you may be overwhelmed by the palpable aroma of fresh flowers during its annual multi-day *Bouquets to Art* exhibit. Flora everywhere, every kind you can imagine and some you've never heard of and couldn't dream up. We go every spring, often with different women tagging along and dragging initially reluctant mates on a MysteryDate.

The concept is uncomplicated: More than 100 hand-picked florists, garden clubs, and individual designers each select a painting or sculpture he, she, or they find inspirational one way or another, and then create a floral homage that will stand in front of or next to the artwork.

Nance gleefully recollects when a designer complemented a Toulouse-Lautrec painting of can-can dancers with white carnations forming the ruffles of what looked like an upside-down dress. Fake legs and dance shoes fancifully stuck into the air.

Baltimore, Boston, Grand Rapids, Milwaukee, and New Orleans have all seen similar exhibits. Though we haven't been to any of those, we *have* expanded our explorations into the world of art-and-plant wonders.

"We're heading for Napa," Nance told me one day, purposefully misleading me to think her MysteryDate would be a tour of several wineries. When we arrived at the di Rosa Center for Contemporary Art, it was impossible to ignore the luscious setting: 217 majestically landscaped acres that encompass vistas of the Napa River, San Pablo Bay, native fauna, and local foliage. But the biggest kick there comes from experiencing, via a too-short

150-minute guided tour, the scope of art at the indoor-outdoor facility.

Until 2019, some 800 California artists had been represented, more than 1,600 works. But then the foundation that ran the center announced its intention to sell off all but 200-400 as "a legacy collection" — so it could keep its doors open.

Since Rene di Rosa had insisted on buying "whatever he liked," a visitor had been apt to see a slideshow of the Chartres Cathedral, a gold-leaf skateboard, a political painting, and a 3-D sculpture of a man with a shoe in his mouth — one right after the other. Life-sized steel cows, a car hanging upside down from a tree, live peacocks squawking and exhibiting their tail feathers, and art cars with rhino heads — such disparate elements fused into a collage of amusement.

The dangling auto, by the way, triggered a memory for me: visiting the Guggenheim Museum in New York City shortly after it opened in 1959. There, on the ground floor at the base of the famed spiral staircase in a building designed by Frank Lloyd Wright sat a naked chrome car bumper attached vertically to a black stone base. Nothing, my memory tells me, apparently had been added or subtracted. No design was etched into the surface. No spots or lines embellished its shiny face. No chips marred the metal. No strings or tags drooped. The title didn't help. "Car bumper," it silently screamed.

"The art world has gone bonkers," I recall saying to a companion.

But now, in my dotage, I somehow find a vehicle suspended from a limb much more acceptable as an art piece. Even with nothing etched on its bumper.

Soul sounds

Know where to find a koto? A kanun? A fipple flute?

They're all musical instruments that have been displayed in a museum in Phoenix, where you can pick, pluck, and pound on many. There you might have found the Steinway upright on which John Lennon composed "Imagine," and a Harmony Sovereign guitar about 10 feet high. "Music is the language of the soul," the MIM (Musical Instrument Museum) founders declare on their website. A collection of 6,500 instruments from 200 countries and territories awaits you in the historical, artistic collection. And you can expect both folk and tribal celebrations to be demonstrated through live and filmed performances in the museum's Music Theatre.

By no means, however, are you limited to jumping off a musical clef for your entertainment. Other special interests may propel you toward the Baseball Hall of Fame in Cooperstown, N.Y., or the Food Museum in New York City. Or, situated in San Antonio, Texas — Barney Smith's Toilet Seat Art Museum. There, in what Tripadvisor has called the wackiest museum in the United States, you'll be informed that the retired plumber had painted and/or engraved at least 1,230 of them. The seats sit, lean, and are piled up.

Runner-up in that Tripadvisor poll was Carhenge, a replica of England's Stonehenge. Located near Alliance, Nebraska, it was built in 1987 by Jim Reinders not from stones but 38 vintage U.S. cars in a circle, each covered with gray spray paint.

If, however, you'd rather witness the trials and tribulations of the Wild West, Wichita's Old Cowtown Museum could top your wanna-see list. It's a 10,000-piece permanent collection in 54 buildings that provide an interactive glimpse of life in a cattle town with Victorian ways in the 1870s. Visitors can hear the blacksmith's anvil and the sound of gunfire in the streets, smell what a farmer's wife is cooking, taste an icy sarsaparilla in the saloon, and feel what it's like to take a stagecoach or wagon ride. Live animals, re-enactors of history, and interpreters are on hand.

Too ordinary for you?

Well, you can always cross the border to snorkel or dive in Cancun, Mexico, a tourist trap/haven where you can see 500 original sunken sculptures at the Underwater Art Museum, the largest such exhibit in the world.

Another destination point south of the border might be the state-owned Museum of the Mummies in Guanajuato, where naturally mummified bodies with grotesque facial expressions were interred during a cholera outbreak in 1833, then disinterred and partially embalmed between 1870 and 1958. Cadavers range from criminals who were buried alive to infants dressed up as saints, an act many Mexicans believe will ensure their passage into heaven. Some 60 corpses are displayed in airtight crypts, out of a 111-body macabre collection that draws more than 4,000 visitors weekly. A few of the mummies still wear the clothes they originally were buried in.

Still not strange enough for you?

Husavik, Iceland, is the site of either a must-see or a must-miss tourist attraction, depending on your taste — the Phallological Museum, with its wide collection of preserved penises and parts of those organs (more than 200) from whales, seals, bears, and other mammals. Including one shriveled human specimen.

From selfies to beefy Bigfoot

The San Francisco Bay Area is home to scores of museums we haven't seen yet but plan to visit (at least a large number of them). They're easy to locate.

A few of the I-can't-believe-there's-a-museum-about-this locales concentrate on amusement-park bits and pieces, antique mechanical toys, computer history, entomology murals, old hand-fans (a treat for the menopausal or manopausal, I'm sure), prison art, Raggedy Ann and Andy, Seabiscuit, semaphores, silent films, teapots, tattoos, and, as might be expected, the Beat generation.

You could even start a bit north with the Charles M. Schulz Museum in Santa Rosa (which has 6,000 original *Peanuts* comic strips, a wall his chair rubbed away when the cartoonist frequently leaned back, and a wall-sized mural of Lucy holding a football for Charlie Brown that's made up of 3,588 comics on ceramic tiles).

The latest fad, in contrast to looking into the way-back machine, is for-profit "selfie museums," sort of art galleries or installations designed to provide settings for visitors to pose in photos for social media sites. Most are "pop-up" exhibits that open for only a few months in a given locale. All tend to feature colorful backdrops, oversized props, and optical illusions. The Color Factory, to cite only one, ran for 8½ months in San Francisco, then shifted to Chicago, Houston, and New York City. Other Instagram museums have included the Dessert Museum, Museum of Ice Cream, Musiquarium, Original Selfie Museum, the Museum of Pizza, and Selfieworld.

As might be expected, in the gay-centric Castro District of San Francisco is a GLBT Historical Society Museum.

You can ignore the fact that the initials don't include every group being included these days, but don't ignore the archives, which are very much up to date. They contain 800 collections of personal papers, photos, recordings, and organizational records — including 1,000 T-shirts, thousands of posters, and 500 oral histories.

Continue to travel in a southerly direction and you'll come to the free Bigfoot Discovery Museum, where lyrics to a Fats Waller tune, "I Love You Baby, But Your Feets Too Big," might make an appropriate theme song. What will you find in that Felton Collection near Santa Cruz? Videos, sound clips, news articles, T-shirts, and toys. What can't you find? Actual evidence (bones or fossils, for instance) of the cryptid's existence.

The venue itself? Smaller than a small bedroom — too tiny, in fact, for an actual Bigfoot to walk around in.

Part 15

Masquerading

These days, when virtually everything's become informal, it usually doesn't matter what you wear. Even on a MysteryDate®.

A minority of women still might prefer being able to strut around in fancy duds, donning jewelry and other accessories sure to make every other woman in the place more than a little bit jealous — especially after applying perfect makeup and making at least one trip to the hairdresser and another to a salon for a mani-pedi.

Decades ago, they called that ritual — then the majority vogue — "getting dressed to the nines." Today, being "cool" has become a purposeful, frequent adaptation of what used to be called Casual Fridays but now has expanded to Mondays, Tuesdays, and the rest of the week (with each day likely to include skin-tight yoga pants or leggings guaranteed to draw a lecher's leer).

To please those females who still derive gratification from getting "gussied up," to use a truly outdated idiom, you need only plan an event that requires some sort of high-fashion statement.

But costuming, in contrast, can *also* be a special treat. That can mean cobbling together somebody-else's vintage this 'n' that from thrift or consignment shops, or yard sales — or utilizing stuff that's been packed away for decades in the recesses of your home and mind. Simply add a dash of daydream and a dot of showmanship.

Such a MysteryDate can take place on Halloween or June 17 (if *that* particular calendar date has some special meaning for you). Or any day at all, just because you feel like it.

Then, you might consider throwing an Oscar Night party where your friends doll up as their favorite movie stars, film characters, directors, or scenario for the current Academy Award year. You could toss in a wacky statuette for each category's best costume. Try it once to see if all goes well; you can always grow the occasion into an annual event.

Or you might throw a pajama party (which needn't involve an actual sleepover) to which you can bring your favorite PJs or robes or nighties (which can be flannel or fuzzy or sexy silk), popcorn or Crackerjacks or other munchies, and group-watch something or other. Adventurous souls might get a kick out of switching nightwear with their partners beforehand for unadulterated fun — or pretend to be a snooping paparazzi by donning some fashonista pajamas and dangling four cameras around your neck.

Recent dress-up fads have included copying costumes from a TV, cable, or streaming series that replicates clothing and manners of a given period (*And Just Like That...* or *The Marvelous Mrs. Maisel*, for example).

And for those who may not be do-it-yourselfers, most communities have rental places where you can obtain costumes ranging from old-timey garments to futuristic outfits.

In short, if you'll pardon an underwhelmingly bad pun, simply suit yourself.

Buckskin, battles, and bottoms

There's no question that costume events make many folks anxious, at least if *their* dressing-up is compulsory. Even on All Saints' Day. But many who are down with dressing down but not with dressing up develop an appetite for apparel when they can be voyeurs.

Texas offers multiple choices of free championship Indian pow wows where, with displays and teepees as a backdrop, tribal dance contests find participants sporting feathers and buckskin, beadwork, and bells.

Maybe, however, you'd rather scrutinize military regalia. The East Bernstadt, Kentucky, reenactments of 1861's Battle of Camp Wildcat provide such an opportunity (spectators as well as those in it are asked to "keep all anachronisms under cover at all times," which I presume means no one should be listening to Lady Gaga or Taylor Swift on an MP3 player or iTunes while fixing a bayonet).

Interesting, indeed, and one of the most outrageous events my research has unearthed — the wife-carrying world championships in Sonkajärvi, Finland. Husbands confront sand and water hazards and must chug a bottle of beer at each stop. The frequently costumed contests include one in which women are handed from one guy to the next. Suma wrestlers and other athletes tend to come up with whimsical ways of toting the females, who must not touch the ground no matter what. Especially in this burgeoning era of feminism and the #MeToo movement, no one's ever permitted to kvetch about getting a woman "off my back."

None of those events happen to be clothing-optional, the opposite end of the dress-up spectrum. But *you* might like to get your butt in gear and head for the Amtrak Mooning Day celebration in Laguna Niguel, California, where thousands have gathered on a designated date each year since 1980 to drop their drawers and flash their rear-ends to each passing train.

And hey, if nudity's your thing, you might travel to a clothes-less World Naked Bike Ride held in 80 cities around the world. Participants parade on two-wheelers, skateboards, and inline skates. Its prime purpose is to have fun while exposing oneself and, its organizers claim, "deliver a vision of a cleaner, safer, body-positive world" in a non-sexual, non-repressed way.

Clowning around

Especially when they involve changing your outfit, theme dates tend to be complicated, complex, and chancy.

They usually have several moving parts — that is, segments in which you travel from one scene to another. They may also involve an added degree of difficulty if you get into a get-up, a notion that causes some skittish folks to wince, squirm, or break out in hives.

Because these kinds of dates require more research and pre-thought than your average bear hug, we rarely initiate them. But when one of us does, the other's usually blown away by all the dots that have been connected.

Since Nancy thrives on jesting, she shouldn't have been surprised when I scheduled a clown date. But she was. We started at a magic shop where I bought two beanies (you know the kind, those mega-cutesy puppies with plastic propeller blades on top). I also purchased red felt noses, one for me, one for her — and theatrical makeup. Stop two was Clown Alley, an eatery not far away; there we faced one another and wolfed down cheeseburgers. While eating, we each put makeup on our partner. Because Nance had been a children's puppeteer for many years, she was good at it; I sucked, so her facial tinting ended up Picasso-esque. Worth a laugh if no blue ribbon.

We then traveled to a waterfront emporium where, typically, clowns and mimes pass hats around. We encountered several singers, a juggler with fire batons, a magician doing card tricks, and a human statue with full body paint. Nary a clown. All the while, two clusters of tourists made throaty noises as if they expected *us* to do something odd and amusing. Instead of accommodating them, we left — to see the final segment of the evening, *The Fool Show*, a one-man theatrical history of clowning starring Geoff Hoyle.

You may choose to sneer at my date, but we'll forever fondly remember it as our not-so-private one-ring circus.

Less intricate was a lowbrow theme date I dubbed All-Star Comedy Nite. It started with me gifting my wife with an antique comic book (a dog-eared, colorful, overpriced second-hand store acquisition about her namesake, Nancy, and that character's cartoonish partner in crime, Sluggo). I handed it to her while wearing Groucho glasses (with *extra*-fuzzy eyebrows and mustache), my only costuming. A funny film was next up, followed by a late-night visit to a comedy club and its lineup of local comics testing new material. The MysteryDate ended at our doorstep when, slightly exhausted, I handed her one of those laughing-box whatchamacallits.

One of Nance's happiest dates was steeped in nostalgia, turning my 2006 junker Camry into a counterfeit time-machine that quickly scooted us back almost a century to the 1920s for a Gatsby picnic. "Wear black pants and a white shirt," was all she'd tell me. We drove to Oakland, an hour from home, and parked around the corner from the Dunsmuir Hellman Historic Estate. My wife popped the trunk and removed my accessories — a straw hat and spats she'd rented from a local costume shop, a polka-dotted bow tie, and her ukulele. In no time at all, I morphed into a chic Sheik from that period. Then she removed a feather headdress to top off the vintage Roaring Twenties outfit she'd been attracted to in a thrift shop years ago for just-this-kind-of-probably-one-time-future-use. She'd been wearing it under a loose-fitting dress to which I'd admittedly paid zero attention.

The *Gatsby Summer Afternoon* is a fundraiser the Art Deco Society's been conducting annually for more than three decades. It lets several hundred afficionados step back into a time when "elegance was a way of life, and the Charleston and foxtrot were all the rage." As the society's website has declared, "This is not a spectator event [but] a stage on which all participants picnic, dance, and sip champagne, reminiscent of a scene from The Great Gatsby, F. Scott Fitzgerald's famous novel of 1925."

Clothing from the '20s to the '40s is a requisite. The dress code bans jeans (torn *or* intact), shorts, polo- and T-shirts, baseball caps (frontwards *or* backwards), sneakers, pantsuits, and any obviously newish clothing.

During the fun-fun-fun event, we reveled in the "Bathing Beauty Revue with the Deco Belles" (pretty damsels clad in vintage one-piece bathing suits who posed for non-stop f-stop photos), though to be honest — even though some might find the idea just the teeniest bit off-color — I'd have rather gawked at gals in more modern teeny bikinis.

In glitzy garb

With a million and a half people within its borders, Philadelphia can easily become a whirlpool of costuming. For over-the-topness, however, its famed annual Mummers Parade takes first place.

The event is a century-old, carnival-like New Year's Day tradition in which 10,000 men and women frolic, pirouette, and strut in lavish costumes made throughout the year especially for the day. Four groups are featured: The garb of one of those components rivals royal attire; another section accentuates string bands strumming on banjoes, saxes, and percussion instruments; a third group produces choreographed theatrical extravaganzas; and the fourth spotlights a batch of men that frequently satirize institutions, issues, and people while clad as wenches.

Rather check out historic costuming of the city? Try the Atwater Kent Museum, a 2,700-item repository for all aspects of local history, including its fashions. The Philadelphia Museum of Art also offers costume exhibits with selections from its storehouse of some 300,000 dresses and other garments, shoes, textiles, and wedding gowns.

Would you rather dine while staring at revelers in glitzy garb? The City Tavern is a reconstructed alehouse (that duplicates a 1773 original) that presents authentic colonial dishes served by staff in period costumes. Special exhibits routinely turn up there — traveling displays (such as the clothing of cabaret dancers at the Moulin Rouge, or Star Trek costumes and props) or semi-permanent ones (such as costumes worn by Philly-born Mario Lanza in his movies).

Austin, Texas, on another hand, has regularly sponsored a '90s dress-up occasion that's celebrated Nirvana, Oasis, the Smashing Pumpkins, the Stone Temple Pilots, Weezer, and other alternative bands. By wearing "long hair, longer goatees, ripped up baggy jeans, and flannel shirts tied around your waist over the flannel shirt you had on as a shirt," you could, according to the town's publicity, relive the days when Eddie Vedder became a bona fide rock star "by singing a song about a kid named Jeremy who liked to draw pictures of mountains with himself on top."

Rather convene unconventionally at a convention? A whole raft of communities in addition to San Diego, home to one of the biggest, have regularly scheduled comic-com and copy-cat assemblies: Atlanta, Austin, Baltimore, Belgium, Denver, St. Louis, Tacoma, Tulsa, Utica, and Wheeling. And on and on and on.

Each December, meanwhile, thousands of partygoers (sometimes called drunks) flood London's streets for an annual SantaCon pub crawl — an event fostered about 40 years ago by an article in *Mother Jones* magazine. Similar events are held in New York City, San Francisco, and Rudolph knows where else.

Then, of course, sheer on-and-off-key joy is possible at sing-along events — some by touring companies — that routinely pull hordes of costumed fans into movie theaters throughout the United States. The *Rocky Horror Picture Show* has long been the most popular, but nipping at the proverbial heels of that film musical's triumphs are melodic go-rounds with *Sound of Music* and *Beauty and The Beast*. And believe it or not, TV's long-dead, super-supernatural trendsetter, *Buffy the Vampire Slayer*, is still alive in sing-along heaven. Most favored reproduction is "Once More, With Feeling," an episode that revolves around a tap-dancing demon who magically forces citizens to sing and dance about their innermost feelings and secrets until they burst into flames.

I can't help but wonder what kind of nonsense the billion-dollar smash hit film, *Barbie*, will eventually spawn since it's apparently already become a cult classic.

In the meantime, for those souls who specifically yearn for a MysteryDate in their hometowns, local newspapers list dress-up activities virtually every month.

Or, of course, you and your partner could go it alone and visit a world-class historical site dressed up in powdered wigs.

Part 16

Hobbies, classes

Despite being middle-aged, Rudy Contratti is still a big kid, one with a major love of life, boundless persistence, and just the right amount of humor.

His hobby is collecting vintage stuff, well more than 75,000 items from the mid-1930s to mid-1970s that cover his walls, ceilings, and doors, artistically cramming the eight small rooms of his house in Fairfax, California, with Americana. Each contains multiple subcategories — ashtrays, figurines, lunchboxes, model trains and small cars and trucks, puppets, rolling pins, and vases, among others. Every piece is an original.

"There's no 're-pop' stuff," he says. "I don't do reproductions."

Rudy invited Nancy to tour his home when she was passing by on a dog-walk one day and asked him about his fences, which are built out of 130 pairs of colorful skis. With his permission, she returned with me in tow — on a MysteryDate®, of course.

Much of Contratti's collection, indoors and out, stems from cross-country "junkin' trips," here-and-there purchases, "and dumpster diving." Each room in his home is, in effect, a self-contained museum. His bedroom, for instance, is a flashback to the heyday of rock 'n' roll and psychedelics.

Ron Henggeler, resident San Francisco hoarder, might also be described as an obsessive gatherer and historian. He confesses his hobby-collection "has gotten out of control, impossible to manage."

The 20-room, five-story Victorian he and three friends own contains "oh, millions of things" stashed in jars and drawers and boxes, and piled everywhere in sight, including jam-packed hallways that guests find almost impossible to pass through. Nance also took me there on MysteryDate, as one of Ron's by-invitation-only visitors, after she'd been offered her first tour as a local historical society rep.

A great source of Henggeler's joy stems from huge olive jars that he rescued from his workplace over decades and now sport decorative tops that he calls "headdresses." What's inside them? "Anything that fits," he says. Like Red Rose tea bags. Ron, a waiter in an upscale eatery who's nearing retirement age and spending more and more time taking professional-quality photographs as another hobby, uses about nine bags of tea every day. When he's finished with each, he pops it into a jar. In another one are Q-tips he's used to clean the ears of his hairless, wrinkled cats. Ron's been pack-ratting since he was a kid (he still has a buffalo skull that his grandfather gave him, childhood Christmas presents, and his original baby blanket), and has been known to jump a fence at night to collect pieces from, let's say, a building from the late 1800s that's being demolished. He readily admits, though, that "all of this stuff is just junk."

Unique MysteryDates? Unquestionably. Trippy? Unquestionably. Delightful? Unquestionably.

It's plain to see that destination points can come into being just because a solo collector's gathered stuff *you* normally wouldn't think of collecting. Consider Litto's Hubcap Ranch. The 360-acre site is in unincorporated Pope Valley (population under 500), which is part of the better-known winery capital of northern California, the Napa Valley. You normally would have gotten there by traveling lots of country roads filled with lots of bumps and potholes, enough to possibly shake loose one or two of *your* hubcaps. True, the roads are covered with asphalt now, but they weren't in 1932 when Emanuel "Litto" Damonte started keeping the ones that got knocked off.

Folklore informs us that when he found his first hubcap, he hung it on the fence so the motorist could find it when he came back. The driver never returned, and when more people lost their hubcaps on the old dirt road, Litto suspended those as well. Passersby, thinking he'd put them there as a design, started bringing him others — or they'd hang some themselves. Before long, an art-installation existed, the shiny hubcaps joining his other shiny objects, tinfoil, and soda cans. The 5,000 hubcaps at the ranch — near the natural springs of Calistoga, half an hour's drive from St. Helena — now comprise a folk-art collection that's been designated as historic state landmark No. 939.

Is Litto's a MysteryDate possibility? Auto-matically!

Obsessions, fixations, addictions

Antoine de Saint-Exupery, author of *The Little Prince*, may have said it best: "Life has taught us that love does not consist of gazing at each other, but in looking outward together in the same direction."

With that emblazoned on your mind, have you — and your mate/spouse/partner/companion/plus-one — seriously been on the lookout for a hobby, avocation, sideline, spare-time waster, or special obsession/fixation/addiction activity you can do collectively? There are roughly 72 thousand to choose from — I counted them one by one (not).

But if you're momentarily stumped, the odds are that hobby shops might be willing to sell *something* you can at least *try out* as a twosome. You might latch onto a pastime that will retain your attention for only an hour or two, but you also might discover an interest that will add richness to your life, hers or his, or both, for decades.

As a duo, you can attend trade shows or expos or swap meets, fly multiple kites at the same time, garden or work on a dual do-it-yourself project, pen poetry or prose or love letters or limericks, put together miniature cars or airplanes (or stuff tiny tall ships into bottles), sail model boats on a lake or take turns steering remote-controlled planes, wash or paint or fix or restore vintage autos or bikes, write a blog or letters of complaint to businesses that "done you wrong" (or complimentary ones to outfits that "done you right").

You also might:
- Get in touch with your inner infant and play hide-and-seek in the store where you once regularly shopped for playthings.
- Deconstruct your ancient photo albums. Go down to your basement or up to your attic or dig through the stuff buried in the hidden recesses of your walk-in closet, and dust off those pages from yesteryear. Try to remember who *that* is, or was, and where the pictures were taken. Aunt Becky when she

was nine? You when you were one and a half? The MysteryDate fun can come when the two of you share reminiscences, or when laughter is evoked by blank stares and blank memories.

- Peruse a how-to book together (alternating pages, maybe). Or write one.
- Make a commitment to a unison project such as scribbling a journal with memories and goals or New Year's resolutions (kept or dismissed). Or create joint greeting cards, or Photoshop family photos into distortedly comic artwork (now called deepfakes, often involving the superimposing of your relatives' heads on the bodies of either buff or gangly movie stars). Skip doing nudies if you want to stay out of trouble.
- If you're both into fresh air, turn that into a hobby and regularly go on environmental excursions. In the spring, you might hike and photograph wildflowers, to cite one option.
- Explore some AI software to see what fantasies the two of you can turn into reality without half trying — and without coming into an artificial conflict with some new law Congress might pass attempting to regulate artificial intelligence.
- Value the sweat and muscles derived from body building? A MysteryDate you might love, then, would be to spot each other while sampling a gym.
- Digitize your free time by turning computer or Xbox or other digitized games into hobby time. See how many you can learn, and how many levels you can achieve. You can alternate who begins and who goes next, or you can try it side-by-side, using two devices. Heightened skin-tingling can come from

3D. And virtual simulated-reality experiences can amp up the pleasure even more (some systems now include tactile sensations labeled "force feedback"). Those who prefer seeing something other than their living rooms or offices can venture to a local arcade/hangout (if you can tolerate the din) and drop a few coins or tokens into the machines. You might even win a tacky stuffed critter.

- Engage yourselves in dueling happy snaps, shooting the same things at the same time (utilizing either camera, smart phone, or both). You can do it almost anywhere (except lockers and shower rooms that law enforcement agents stake out with regularity) — monthly, bi-annually, or once.

You also could consider redoing an activity you or your partner used to engage in long ago (as youngsters, maybe) and might enjoy as an adult (chronologically speaking, of course).

Like so many other choices in this book, none of these depend on where you reside. We're now in an era in which digital devices and countless apps can put us in touch with endless prospects almost anywhere around the nation or world. Tiny towns as well as crowded cities offer an astounding variety of selections.

Grinnell, Iowa, with a hair over 9,000 residents, can serve as a good illustration. It's home to a college with an admirable 9-to-1 student-faculty ratio and to Iowa Valley Community College, which offers continuing-ed programs and business training. Special classes are available, too, at the Spaulding Center for Transportation, which has multiple items that delve into the arenas of aviation, engineering, heavy equipment manufacturing, highway construction, and trucking.

Your community will have its own, individual history and agenda, for sure. And so will you. All there for the asking.

Lessons from a to z

Craving to acquire new knowledge, share it with your partner, turn it into a MysteryDate? Easy-peasy. Check out classes. In real or digital time. Then enroll together as a MysteryDate for a single session or a series.

Consider taking a course in body painting, computer or motivational skills, dancing, drama, fencing, first aid or life-saving techniques, magic, photography, or window-washing. Or *whatever* tickles your joint fancies.

CPR classes — "hero-training" (typically given at fire stations, hospitals, and through the Red Cross) — can be a tangible way to demonstrate to your family, friends, or mate that you care about them. Might there be foreign-language studies in your near future? Maybe you'd prefer to stimulate your history memory-banks by learning what we've partially overcome politically and militarily with a session or two on Civil War clashes. And you could later add a second part to the MysteryDate by visiting the locales involved.

In a similar vein, you could delve into how ruins became ruins, foreign (Pompeii or Machu Picchu, for example) or domestic (the 160-acre Lovers Leap State Park in New Milford, Connecticut, which provides a panoramic view of industrial remains). That Lovers Leap, you'll discover by the way, can offer hiking trails, scenic vistas, paved parking, *and* the spot where a legendary tragedy supposedly took place. Some believe the Pootatuck Indian Chief Waramaug's daughter, Princess Lillinonah, and her lover jumped to their deaths there.

If that tale's too much of a downer, you might prefer a classroom backstory about the remnants of a pyramid-shaped tower originally built on the peak of Bear Mountain, in Salisbury, Connecticut, in 1885. The structure, constructed with 350 tons of stone, slowly deteriorated, and ultimately collapsed. A plaque that had been perched on it was destroyed and a new one was permanently set into the rubble half a century ago — despite it containing faux info about the mount being the highest in the state.

Still unsatisfied? Well, you could take a crack at aerospace studies, astronomy, Bible studies, birthing (which has *nothing* to do with where Donald Trump claimed Barack Obama was born), creative writing, decorating cupcakes, film and television, history of the pig in America (specifically at Xavier University, perhaps), low-carb dieting, Native American studies, the science of superheroes (at the University of California at Irvine, for instance), statistics, war-craft, Yiddish, yoga, and zombies in popular media (at Columbia College, at least).

Added opportunities? How about learning more about antiquing, beachcombing, bead-working, beer-brewing or wine-making, body-building, bonsai-tree growing, calligraphy, candle-making, card-playing, ceramics and pottery, coin or stamp or trading-card collecting, crocheting, doll-making, family-tree tracing, film-making, gaming (sometimes pejoratively referred to as gambling — or betting the family farm), higher math, an insider's view of circuses or rodeos, inline skating, internet or television surfing, jewelry-making, needlepoint, paint-balling, people-watching, photography, puzzling, quilting, robotics, scrapbooking, skateboarding, skeet shooting, submarine-building, treasure-hunting, or zucchini-cooking?

Wow! And that doesn't count the other million or so pay-as-you-go or free choices available at local night schools, community colleges, recreation departments, and private institutions. In auditoriums, libraries, and at least 306,497 other spots that I counted one by one (not).

If you can think of it, there's undoubtedly somebody teaching it somewhere. And free catalogues appear every which way you turn, in ample quantities and sufficient heft to make your eyes and mind explode — or at least blur — if you're not careful.

Don't want to leave the warmth of your home? No problem. Sign up, instead, for a not-for-credit, just-for-pleasure, correspondence-on-online course together. You might consider one that'll teach you to write a memoir or autobiography (with or without using AI), or one through which you can be altruistic or self-sacrificing by taking a class your partner's apt to like more than you.

Part 17

Performances

Music's available in just about every place you can contemplate. And you don't have to travel to Cuba or spend gobs of cash to hear it, sing it, play it, or dance to it. And I'm talkin' live here, not Deezer or Pandora. All it takes is a craving to be entertained, checking out a few blogs or newspapers or posters, doing a scintilla of additional research, (maybe) grunting as you get off the couch and unplug that flatscreen, and (maybe) grunting again as you climb into your car (or truck or RV) or hop onto a tandem bike or electric scooter.

Many cafes and restaurants have live music that let you cheerfully hum with your hummus or tap your toes while tasting tea. Nancy and I have even been on walks in the park and serendipitously come across jam sessions with drums, duos, guitars, large and small groups.

Sometimes, I know, there's music in your head (via earworms) or in your ears (with the help of buds), pleasing you as you walk or ride. But it's also *out there*, beyond your skull, in nooks and crannies you normally don't consider.

Consider, for instance, a trio we experienced at the Harmony Sweepstakes, an annual a cappella concert, at a college near us. Most of the cabaret-style singing groups were in top form, with tight instrument-less vocal harmonies, an eclectic repertoire, and an ability to vocalize in numerous musical styles. At the time of our MysteryDate®, one was celebrating 30 years of being on stage together, though each of the threesome had separate, successful day-jobs. So, when Nance learned they were later performing nearby, free, outdoors, and in the summertime, it was a no-brainer. She asked a couple of friends to join us for the concert and for dinner afterward. The MysteryDate worked like — oh, you know — a harmonious charm.

Another time, we couldn't help grinning as we watched kids dance at a street fair with their parents and whirl around with lengthy, colorful May Day-type ribbons. I sipped Diet Pepsi; she nursed her latte. We both drank in the melodies. And sopped up the sun's rays. The only challenge was finding a good place to sit (which we did, though a medium-sized bush had its way with us part of the time).

For Nance, music has been a creative thread forever. It started when she was three, sitting at the piano with her father every night playing songs from the '20s and '30s and '40s. He'd been a professional jazz musician who'd played sax with big-band outfits like the Dorsey Brothers, Peter Duchin, and Paul Whiteman, and so she eventually learned *all* the Cole Porter, George Gershwin, and show tunes he knew — by ear. Although disrupted by the pandemic, she still performs on occasion, exclusively in senior centers now, and those tunes remain a major part of her repertoire.

Because I've long known how much my musical-junkie wife loves almost any kind of jazz performance, that's given me a major fallback MysteryDate category, a mental default position to rely on when I momentarily can't think up something we haven't already tried. As a result, I've taken her over the years to an extraordinary number of concerts by jazz soloists, trios, and quartets (as well as to performances of big bands, symphonies, and operas — and that doesn't count experimental music on bizarre instruments). She's taken me as well.

Why am I telling you this? Because it illustrates how and where you might focus on a daydream, hobby, or occupation, and use it as the basis of a MysteryDate. Such events can certainly include your buddy, kid, mother-in-law, parent, or partner. Or all the above.

Meanwhile, don't forget your community theater, drama class, or YMCA or YWCA. High schools are good venues, too (we once marveled at 13- to 15-year-old actors embodying gangster roles in *West Side Story*).

You also can buy or download or learn tunes you can play again. And again. Nance once did just that — admittedly to excess — with *Guys & Dolls*, her all-time favorite musical. Before we drove to a revival of the show, she listened to the score on earphones while walking our pooch, then played it on the piano when I was out. She also sang most of it in the car on the way, an action that led me to correctly guess where we were heading on the MysteryDate she'd programmed. During the live show, as I might have predicted, she hummed quietly along with the cast (softly enough to *not* disturb those seated around us). And that, as unbelievable as it sounds, was followed by her singing it one more time on the way home.

It's probable that she'll do something exactly like that again when we go to the next performance of the show in our area.

Another of our most memorable outings to an onstage musical was to Baz Luhrmann's stage production of

Moulin Rouge, where I spent too much time stargazing at a gaunt Nicole Kidman, seated manikin-like on the aisle opposite us. "Does she ever breathe?" I whispered at one point.

Yet another unforgettable musical experience was *Into the Woods*, because Nance's convertible Beetle Cabriolet was stolen from a street near the theater and disappeared either "into the woods" or the ozone.

Nothing was stolen, thank goodness, when I scheduled a MysteryDate in the 55-acre San Francisco Botanical Gardens, where a dozen pianos had been placed for the public to play over a 12-day period during an event titled *Flower Piano*. Should you go, don't expect perfectly tuned, new Bösendorfer or Steinway pianos. Dean Mermell, one of the two artists who conceived it, expounded on the project to the *San Francisco Chronicle*: "They're not concert-level... They're not really good enough to sell but they're not in bad enough shape to throw out." Truth be told, some have had one or two keys that are sticky or loose. And maybe a malfunctioning pedal. But they still could resonate with lovely tunes. Surprisingly, the Saturday we went, we ran across no keyboard-hoarders. Everyone who wanted to play got a chance — including my wife, who toyed with all 88 keys of five different instruments.

My wife contends she's been extremely lucky having me guide her along a happiness-filled musical path that began almost 70 years ago when we were teens and I familiarized her with many jazz performers in Manhattan. Those, of course, pre-dated our MysteryDates by many years. The only mystery back then was if we'd end up as a couple. Luckily, we agree, we did.

Music, maestro, please

Your musical tastes most likely will veer from ours. So, regardless of what your performance palates are, here are a few notes you might want to hit:

- Curl up and listen to your partner's favorite music (presuming he or she's not totally into rap while you're totally into classical, or vice versa). Consider adding posters or memorabilia as gifts.
- Dance up a perfect storm. Select from ballroom, hip-hop, Irish clog, rock, salsa, square-dancing, swing, or Western.
- Create some body percussion a la Bobby McFerrin while jointly listening to rhythmic tunes you both like.
- Make a melodic playlist to enjoy together while tapping into iTunes, Spotify, YouTube, or whatever turns you on.
- Volunteer at a concert or score some passes.

In addition, you might try sing-along activities that take place all over the world in *your* style (blues, chorale, classical, country, folk) — especially Messiah events from Belfast to Brooklyn, Oakland to Ottawa, Portland to Paris. The San Francisco Sinfonietta annually performs "Handel's Sing It Yourself Messiah" at the historic Dolores Basilica a few weeks before Christmas, for instance. The evening is "interactive" and paced by the conductor of a symphony (who leads both choral group and audience).

Even in American's tinier villages, there are plenty of musical possibilities. Look, for instance, at Fredericksburg, Virginia, a town of about 19,000. Click on a one-month online calendar and you'll find a slew of potential MysteryDates, with karaoke being the most popular. Available, too, is live bluegrass *and/or* big band, blues, country, jazz, liturgical, rock, salsa, and swing.

Summerfest, billed as the world's largest music festival, takes place on about a dozen stages along Milwaukee's Lake Michigan shore — and pulls about a million watcher/listeners over 11 days who attend more than 1,000 performances by 800 acts. In contrast, because it's limited to a single musical genre, is the Gospel Music Festival in Rockport, Texas. Although it draws a decidedly narrower audience, it gets enthusiastic people from all over the United States. And in Shreveport, Louisiana, the four-day Mudbug Madness festival features Cajun-Zydeco music on the main stage, rhythm 'n' blues and jazz on the Swamp stage, and stuff for the young 'uns on the kids' stage. Gumbo and fried 'gator top the food list. Sidelights include crawfish-eating and calling contests.

Want something even more removed from the norm? I'd wager that *your* community probably has a few tidbits that I haven't learned about — yet.

I did love one I'd never even heard about before, thanks to a Nance-driven MysteryDate: the Audium, aka the Theatre of Sound-Sculptured Space. Visitors sit in the dark and experience the "sound-space continuum" coming at them from every direction at unpredictable times, from speakers in sloping walls, a floating floor, and a suspended ceiling. Compositions in the 49-seat theater, according to one of Audium's creators, Stan Shaff, are performed live by a tape conductor who directed the sounds "through a custom-designed console to any combination of 176 speakers." Audiences, he explains, "should feel sound as it bumps up against them, caresses, travels through, covers, and enfolds them."

Easy does it

Stage performances, obviously, are among the easiest MysteryDates to set up: Decide what you'll both enjoy, buy tickets, and get to the theater. To include others, simply purchase more tickets. Often you can obtain them for less through online discounters or walk-in, cut-rate outlets. And so-called "rush" tickets sometimes become available for those willing to stand in line at the box office at the last minute. We fondly remember, despite *not* being opera buffs, waiting in long line for standing-room-only places in Vienna to see a huge cast in *The Tempest.*

Performances can be experimental or regular. Premiere or revival. Light as grandma's favorite soufflé or as heavy as a Tolstoy tome. Personal taste, to sort of repeat myself, is the only arbiter. And speaking of taste, some theaters routinely offer complimentary wine or soft drinks (accompanied at opening night receptions by dainty morsels or less-dainty pizza).

Being in the right place at the right time can affect a date, too. You can, for example, create what we've called a "tack-on" or "added-value" MysteryDate — when you've already scheduled one but insert, append, or attach another element. Nance, for instance, squeezed in a special surprise meal between one of her own performances near our home and a show I'd booked. Not that long ago she added a yacht club event only two hours before a non-MysteryDate opening night show I'd been slated to cover as a newspaper critic. Eating her surreptitiously packed sandwiches in the car meant we were able to do both, catch up with a few folks we hadn't seen in more than a quarter of a century, and then watch a handful of boats sail by.

No matter where you reside, in a crowded city or sparsely populated duchy, performances pop up everywhere. All the time.

Here are a couple of basics to perhaps help you:
- No real rules exist, so just pick *your* favorite — comedy or tragedy — and enjoy it, indoors or out.
- Don't like sitting that long? Try going onstage and performing yourself, perchance even *with* your partner.

And I can virtually guarantee that, without exerting a great deal of energy, you won't have to travel too far to catch burlesque, circuses (from top Cirque du Soleil pros to amateur local yokels), classic or contemporary dramas or musicals, horse or dog or alligator shows, novelty acts, one-man (or woman) routines, stand-up or sit-down comics, or a variety of variety programs. Flavor to your taste. Then, as the saying goes, rinse and repeat.

It goes without saying (even though we're saying it), megalopolis areas have the broadest entertainment mélange. If you're visiting the Greater New York vicinity, for example, the Big Apple itself will offer a Big Assortment — the Lincoln Center, the Metropolitan Opera, the N.Y.C. Ballet, countless shows on and off and off-off Broadway, plus myriad clubs with unlimited music you can hum or dance to.

Going somewhere else? Minneapolis, for instance, has the Guthrie Theater, with its resident company that draws some folks in tuxedos, others in jeans. Dig into your own hometown's offerings, however, and you'll find performance possibilities all over the map: civic centers, farmers' markets, inns, open mics, restaurants, street corners, subways.

And for any readers still a tad depressed by what little's in their wallets, free shows still are alive and well.

Part 18

Mental wellness

MysteryDates® for Nancy and me periodically involve altered consciousness — although for us that means, rather than a state brought on by hallucinogenic drugs, falling into the now-clichéd category of folks who "get high on life." Having a massage tops my list of guilty pleasures, one in which the physical activity leads to improving my mental health.

Every now and then, my back and shoulders insist on strong hands pressing into sore muscles, an impetus for ecstatic groans and comments like, "That hurts so good." Nance's feelings are identical, but she experiences them much more frequently. So, after one of her most comforting sessions ever, she thought, "If I love it this particular masseuse this much, I'll bet Woody would, too." Voila! MysteryDate!

She told me to be ready for a date after a home-cooked dinner. So, I showered and dressed, fully expecting to go out. No way. Shortly after the body worker rang the doorbell, I had to take my clothes off. Nance quietly headed down the staircase to our bedroom as the woman put on some pacifying music and I climbed onto her table in our living room upstairs. Within seconds, I was letting out oohs and ahhs. And a few restful sighs. I later experienced, as a bonus, a good night's sleep.

It was a rarity — a one-sided MysteryDate in which one partner's delight was derived solely from the other's — but hardly the only one we've ever experienced.

Once, when I was "tied up in knots" about a work situation, Nance believed she could help me with a MysteryDate encounter of the mystical kind. Years before, when she was being treated for breast cancer, she'd been gifted with several guided-imagery sessions as part of a healing package. She'd found them surprisingly helpful — soothing mostly. She expected I would, too. So, she drove me to the specialist's office, sat in the waiting room and meditated (to loosen herself up, cost-free) while I let my inner man-in-knots be replaced by Tranquil Man.

The gamut and the gray matter

There are incalculable other activities, some involving physical effort, that can create good mental health. They can run a gamut from regular exercise (Pilates, push-ups, tai chi, or yoga) to dietary drills (eating more fruits and veggies, giving up caffeine, or ingesting less alcohol and carbonated drinks, carbs, salt, and sugar). The requisite to setting up one of those as a MysteryDate? Merely using your resourceful gray matter.

A handful of folks we know regularly take a blank book into the woods to write poetry about what they experience, or sketch, or simply jot down all the special things they see (a leaf in the shape of a heart, for example), an easy discipline that connects their brain to their heart.

You also might count on being mentally pampered by beauty spas, double-bubble baths, hair styling, hot tubs, his-and-hers' facials or mani-pedis, or the old-faithful saunas.

Other choices might be affirmations, discussion groups on a galaxy of topics (books, films, needlepoint), going to coffee or lunch with a friend, political activism (phone-calling from home or a so-called "boiler room," attendance at meetings or rallies), positive thinking, religious assemblies, taking a leisurely walk with the dog (yours or your neighbor's), therapy of innumerable stripes that will never require your working up even a minor sweat (including art, drama, and music), and volunteering.

You could always, if so inclined, try a joint shopping excursion for exercise equipment, which doesn't have to involve a $20,000 gym setup but can be as ordinary as a huge stability ball to roll your back on, a jump rope, or a tiny trampoline.

Sometimes, it's clear, less *is* more.

Bang the drum hypnotically

Whenever Nance hears music, she normally taps out time with a foot, hand, fingers, ring — whatever's handy. But she'd never played the drums. Nor had I when she arranged the date.

There thrives in San Rafael, minutes from our home, a store with a modest name, Open Secret Bookstore, but an unwieldy add-on title, Music and World Art Galley and Rainbow Body Cultural Center. It specializes in all things spiritual, including occasional drumming sessions.

Percussionist Gabriel Harris, son of folksinger Joan Baez, ran the show the evening we attended. His group, Bogofusion (which he called "the global customizable party band"), had played for President Bill Clinton, billionaire Microsoft magnate Bill Gates, and actor

Harrison Ford, and had opened for Stevie Wonder and Elvis Costello.

Nance had known none of that. What she *had* known was that he'd scheduled a drum session in which participants could play one or more multi-cultural drums — and be coached, encouraged, and taught by him and members of his group. My wife certainly hadn't expected to see his world-class entertainer-mom drumming and dancing with her young grandchild in her arms. But that happened, too. Which proves you can't quite predict who or what you'll encounter on a MysteryDate.

At any rate, we chose our drums and immediately began experimenting with them. The lesson started a few minutes later, with straight-ahead beats and techniques involving palms and fingers. "This is really uncomplicated and easy — and hypnotic," I said. A split second after I uttered those jinxed words, complex polyrhythms wafted into the air, led by the band and a few members of the public who'd attended previous sessions. "Whoa," I said to myself. "We're newcomers." But somehow, slightly embarrassingly, I'd said it aloud. "Let's stick to the basic stuff — it'll blend in," Nance whispered in my left ear.

At the end of the session, our hands stung a little, but my heart was wide open, having accepted the teaching that the drumming opens spirits and minds to connections with others.

Yet another MysteryDate — mine, this time — involved lengthier tapping (and marching) to different drummers.

For the uninitiated, Taiko is a style that began in Japan 1,400 years ago, though the modern outgrowth dates back only to the 1950s. Nance hadn't heard of the practice, but, given her love for almost all things musical, I took a calculated risk on setting up a MysteryDate in Berkeley anyway — an all-day concert-celebration. When my wife found out what was in store for her, she expressed fear that sitting through hour upon hour of huge, large drums banging in her brain would drive her bonkers (even though, obviously, we could leave any time we so desired). But she was wrong, as I'd presumed. She loved every beat.

The drums come in many sizes, but many are bigger than the players (men primarily, due to the strength required to pound on the instruments).

A baby cradled right in front of us peacefully slept through the entire afternoon performance because, we found out later, the drumbeats connected with his heartbeats. And ours.

A scoop about poop

Whether participants are mentally well or mentally ill may depend on your vantage point as well as reality, but the No Pants Subway Ride in New York City has been growing in popularity despite it being on a different date in January and in a different locale each year. What started as a seven-guy prank has morphed into a 5,000-person phenomenon (dare I call it a craze?) — and has spread to 60 cities in almost 30 countries (from Latvia to Tokyo). Tens of thousands apparently participated in a recent New York flash mob. I have yet to drop my drawers, but the sheer number and sheer underwear make me pant with merriment.

Perhaps, though, mental health for you will depend instead on doing some good in the world. Like helping the environment. For example, do you abhor the graffiti in your town? Bugged by weeds or poison oak in your neighborhood or nearby parks? Tired of tripping over garbage on the sidewalks or in the roadways, or finding cigarettes, other litter, or dog poop on the ground? With just a little initiative, you can feel better by helping create a more pristine environment *during* a MysteryDate. Nance planned a cleanup — washing several filth-caked cars in our cul de sac — with friends. When finished, each of us was convinced he or she'd done something good while having fun (after spritzing each other).

The cost? Whatever soap and water we used in the shower at day's end.

Pick your passion

Good mental health, many pundits maintain, may be dependent on good spiritual health. But that doesn't mean you must be born into or convert to a particular religion — or even regularly attend a specific service or gathering that lifts your consciousness. Often, I believe, it's not only where you live physically and spiritually but your willingness to hear the tenets of others.

Balance, serenity, and even holiness may await you *if* you're interested. It's possible to bump into them at a retreat in the boonies of Arkansas or North Carolina (or you fill in the blank), in a therapy group in the Ozarks, in a yurt in Omaha. "Seek and ye shall find" is my pilfered instruction.

Yes, you can sample Baha'i, Buddhism, Christianity, Confucianism, Gnosticism, Hinduism, Islam, Judaism, Magic, Paganism, Polytheism, the Rastafari movement, Scientology, Sikhism, Taoism, Unitarian Universalism, Voodoo, or Witchcraft or any of the thousands of other faiths, sects, or splinter groups.

Your MysteryDate can explore alternate planes or *this* world, atheism, and/or Edgar Cayce, holistic healing practices, miracles, near-death experiences, past-lives therapy, pseudo-scientific data, religious rituals, or your inner Goddess.

Like Socrates, you alone (or in conjunction with your mate) get to pick your passion — or your salvation.

Natural MysteryDates

Fully immersing yourselves in nature may result not only in improved physical health but mental wellness as well.

Consider, for instance, a Gunsel Horse adventure in either the Black Hills and badlands of South Dakota, or Yellowstone, whose natural wonderment exists mainly in Wyoming but also juts into Montana and Idaho. There, four-, seven-, or 10-day horse trips thrust you back in time to when you could be in a saddle for days and never see a fence. Though I'm encouraging these activities, I hereby categorically disclaim responsibility for any potential saddle-soreness.

Dude ranches — in a variety of places where you can attend rodeos, hunt, learn rope tricks and skills, or just plain ride — are slightly more tame nature possibilities. But there's also the possibility of a road trip along the California coastline's Big Sur, where visitors often say they're left speechless by the high cliffs and the surf that pounds against them (the cliffs, that is, not the travelers).

Calaveras County, also in California, is famous because of Mark Twain's 1867 short story about the "celebrated jumping frog." The "jump" — with as many as 2,000 amphibian entrants — is now an annual extravaganza, part of a multi-day jubilee that draws more than 45,000 tourists.

Instead of thinking small, maybe you'd rather watch gentle giants that happen to live on (or are visiting) either coast. Just pencil in a whale watching MysteryDate. Most guidebooks will help locate where they mate and have their babies, migrate, sing and whistle, and hang out. And flip. Different species of whales can often be found, among other places, in Boston, Cape Cod, Santa Barbara and Seattle — and spots as far apart as Africa, Alaska, the Azores, Maui, Melbourne, the Mexican Riviera, and Vancouver.

Too limited because you wish to study *multiple* varieties of water life? Simply visit the famed Galapago Islands, where you can play a compelling game of "I spy" while focusing on boobies, cormorants, frigate birds, giant tortoises and marine turtles, marine iguanas, penguins, sea lions, and an abundance of underwater creatures.

Want, instead, to check out *enclosed* areas? Just select one of the thousands of nature preserves throughout the world, conservation areas that protect fauna and flora. Some are game reserves, others are marine parks; many are wildlife areas that have become safety nets for bears, birds, elephants, leopards, tigers, and wolves. They're overseen by national governments, research organizations, or charities, and may offer birding, boating, camping, fishing, hiking, and ecological activities.

And at Safari West in Santa Rosa, 400 exotic mammals and birds roam free in their natural habitat on a private wildlife preserve for endangered species. You'll find African spoonbills, antelopes, lemurs, nyalas, ostriches, wildebeests and, more likely than not, several exotic species you probably never heard of. You can stay overnight (in tents that have beds, electric blankets, hardwood floors, and handmade wooden furnishings). And they've offered special programs on the full moon, Thanksgiving, and New Year's Eve — plus a Friday Night girls' getaway as well as "Watusi weekdays" that promise a romantic time in luxury tents with chocolate, Swedish massages, and wine.

If you like to envision critters in formal attire, you can check out penguins in the Antarctic. You could pass them on a cruise ship or specifically take a voyage during breeding season. Alternatively, you could just go to a local zoo and observe them in a temperature-regulated room at feeding time.

Zoos, of course, are always an easy-to-arrange MysteryDate with a couple of acquaintances, groups of friends, kids, or for a special party. You can stroll along at your own pace, or, at many venues, rent a handheld audio device that guides you through and provides behind-the-scenes tales of behavioral training. Most zoos also program special moments — carts filled with "touchables" (fur, bones, teeth, etc.), feeding frenzies for critters, and fund-raising luncheon frenzies for patrons.

The Atlanta facility goes one better. It offers Family NightCrawlers, where groups go "backstage" after hours, then spend an overnight crammed with breakfast, exclusive tours, games, and a scavenger hunt.

To turn W.C. Fields' classic movie line on its head, an event like that can become "a fit night out for man *and* beast."

Part 19

Conversations, lectures, sermons

One of Nancy's icons is the late songwriter-composer-lyricist Stephen Sondheim. So, when he'd booked a rare, staged conversation only an hour away from us, my MysteryDate® gland started throbbing uncontrollably.

My wife saw ads for the gig and wanted to go but I made lame excuses about ticket prices being too high ("especially since none of his *music* will be featured") and the travel distance being too far. She didn't guess I had something up my MysteryDate sleeve: After all, she trusted my judgment.

I'd long known the film-festival director who was going to interview the musical legend. So, I hoped I could score some comps. Which I did. But not until the absolute last minute. The upshot — suddenly I had to become a quick-turnaround artist, first finding a responsible babysitter for our granddaughter, who'd been weekending with us. Then I had to get Nance to concoct a super-fast dinner we could inhale, ready the kid for bed, and get dressed to go. All within an hour. She did it, with five minutes to spare. And all I'd had to say was, "Sweetheart, I need you to do something you've never done before: Do whatever I tell you to do, without question."

Amazing! Years of building untested trust finally paid off.

Regrettably, because I'd been to the auditorium only once before, my frenzy led me to turn off the freeway too early. As soon as I realized my wayward ways, I doubled back. But time was exceptionally tight, so I was getting exceptionally uptight. We made it, albeit a bit breathlessly — with a whole 60 seconds to waste.

Nance was thrilled she got to see and hear her idol, who smoothly regaled us with untold tales about his childhood and early professional years. But the cost of the freebie was too high. Next time I'll pay the price of admission early on and avoid all the last-minute anxiety.

Yuck's in the beholder's eye

"Lecture." Does the word imply yuckiness to you? Elitism? Or maybe worse yet, boredom?

You have the power to turn the negativity inside out, of course, because how a lecture will strike you depends on who's talking, how the material is presented, your interest level, and how much time and energy you want to expend. Think, too, about the almost infinite variations of onstage or offstage dialogues. You can, for instance, attend a panel discussion. Or an interview or debate. With two individuals or half a dozen. On virtually any subject in the world.

Surely, *some* topic must interest you (and your partner) enough to hear somebody with expertise rant about it.

Since the range of face-to-face chats, lectures, podcasts, and online chat-room conversations is unbelievably broad, think for a microsecond about your avocations, curiosities, dreams. Then scope out a cable TV cooking demo, a casual talk at your neighborhood library or bookstore, a digital dialogue, a humane-society exchange that focuses on your favorite breed of animal, a local PBS tête-à-tête, a one-shot art gallery discussion, a surfing-equipment store where experts can wax decidedly un-poetic about your favorite board, or a do-it-yourself shop that slates talk after talk on how to...

Whatever jiggles your neck wattle.

Your last step, of course, is conning your mate into joining you. Come to think of it, you could even curl up on your couch together and sense each other's blood pressure rise as some demented but entertaining radio talk show extremist turns reality upside down.

Don't want to limit yourself to a twosome? Easily altered: Just invite your cerebral or wine-sipping, mountain-climbing buddies and have a MysteryDate for four, or seven, or...

Mindful listening

A friend, a life coach, once showed me how to relax, unwind, and find quietude through "walking meditations" and "mindfulness." I wasn't disciplined enough, so neither took. As a result, I'm still occasionally un-relaxed and wound-up, nowhere near the vicinity of calm.

But on one particularly agitated day, I chose to try again — by using a technique I'd come to label "mindful listening." I decided to check out a San Francisco sermon by an exiled Vietnamese Zen Buddhist monk, Thich Nhat Hahn, who, in addition to being a lecturer, quadrupled as author, peace activist, and teacher. Nance, who's normally a pragmatist, intermittently explores mystical arenas, so I gauged that it would make a good MysteryDate. I'd read only one of the speaker's thin books on meditation but the thought of being in his presence at the majestic Grace Cathedral, known for its open-minded attitudes and practices (especially an acceptance of teachings from a variety of faiths), was more than slightly appealing — despite, due to our not being particularly spiritual on a day-to-day basis, being a bit intimidating.

Nance didn't know Thich Nhat Hahn was coming to town so she couldn't understand why we were parking on Nob Hill. No problem. I knew that since both of us had been peace activists during the Vietnamese War, and since the expatriate had established medical centers, founded and rebuilt bombed villages, resettled homeless families during that war, set up schools, and influenced Martin Luther King to oppose the battle, we'd both find him inspirational. And comforting.

He was.

Perma-smiles were etched onto our faces as he proposed — poetically — non-violent solutions to conflict. But it truly wasn't his politics that soothed us; it was his turn-the-other-cheekness.

Afterward, we walked one of the labyrinths found both in the church's courtyard and its interior — circles within circles that can quickly thrust a visitor who walks them into a meditative state. For us, that prospect paralleled the lecture. Bottom line when we finished: We felt serene. Centered. Mindful.

And we later thought about those with different religious perspectives, philosophies, or world views than we live by. For them, we knew, countless lectures, prayer sessions, and sermons were available. They could easily select a different MysteryDate at a church social or midnight service, volunteer together for a mosque or synagogue project, watch a televangelist or listen to a radio preacher. Or go on a retreat, enroll in Bible or Torah or Koran studies as a team, or attend a revival meeting or gospel concert.

"Seek and ye shall find" is my pilfered instruction.

Yes, you can sample Baha'i, Buddhism, Christianity, Confucianism, Gnosticism, Hinduism, Islam, Judaism, Magic, Paganism, Polytheism, the Rastafari movement, Scientology, Sikhism, Taoism, Unitarian Universalism, Voodoo or Witchcraft or any of the thousands of other faiths, sects, or splinter groups.

Our base, the San Francisco Bay Area, gets a bad rap as hedonistic, irreligious and woke (whatever that means), despite it being the home of hundreds and hundreds of houses of worship and faith-based groups. Still, those seeking an away-from-home religious MysteryDate might feel better visiting Los Angeles, where 40 percent of the city's 4.4 million residents are Catholic; New York, where 2 million Jews live in the metropolitan area and the concentration of Muslims is highest (with half a million); or Salt Lake City's metro area of 1.1 million that caters to Mormons (a name now officially replaced by the more formal Church of Jesus Christ of Latter-day Saints).

Checking out a place of worship in any one of those locales during a special holiday might constitute a particularly fascinating MysteryDate. But visiting *any* spiritual place you're unfamiliar with could be exhilarating.

I once initiated a string of MysteryDates to services neither or us had attended before. They included such settings as Baha'i, Gnostic, Christian Science, Jews for Jesus, 7th Day Adventist, and Sikh. One of the most fascinating was at the Sanctuary of the Holy Shekinah.

It was all so cinematic — and, unexpectedly, so sexual. The room itself could have been a set plucked from a Fellini movie. Bordello pinks and roses tinted its walls and ceiling; the aroma of incense tickled our nostrils. As the high priestess whispered a prayer, her breasts threatened to leap from the V-neck of her sackcloth robe. References to the bridal chamber, virginity, and the womb punctuated the liturgy.

Bishop Rosamonde Ikshvàku Miller, robed founder of the sect that's been in existence four decades, utilized every fragment of her alluring voice, French accent, and veneer of mystery. She managed to blend — with surprising ease — Gnostic thought, kabbalistic mysticism, Latin phrases, and the psychological explorations of Carl Jung. Not to mention the stubborn conviction that she's part of a direct apostolic line of succession to secrets first revealed by Mary Magdalene.

As her service unfolded, several women assumed the role of choir, one or two at a time. One particular solo was jarring — it referred to women being both virgin and whore.

We felt, at times, like spiritual voyeurs.

And although she insisted the sanctuary's not "a crazy California church," the service left a decidedly different aftertaste than standard-issue religion. Yet oddly serene.

Being straight with the queers

In many metropolitan areas, queers — adults who identify as lesbian, gay, bisexual, queer, or trans — represent a healthy small chunk of the population. San Francisco tops that list with a little over 6 percent — twice the national average, according to a Gallup poll. But because the city's metro area isn't nearly as big as its notoriety, that only translates to 95,000 people. In sheer numbers, New York's way ahead — with about 273,000.

Nance and I typically attend events that have absolutely zero to do with sexual orientation (or, tangentially, being black or Hindu or bipolar). Because we're both flaming heterosexuals, we tend to set up what some of our handful of non-straight friends label "het" MysteryDates (using gay shorthand for heterosexual). Now and then, though, we venture into primarily gay neighborhoods, where we've recurrently encountered endless friendly LGBTQ+ folk.

When my wife heard about a program the San Francisco Museum and Historical Society was presenting about the Castro, an area long the center of gay life in the city, it triggered her curiosity. That led, naturally, to her impromptu MysteryDate: A three-person panel discussion with participants who were accepting, bright, funny, and warm — and extremely candid during their conversation about their feelings. They enlightened us and the other listeners about same-sex struggles and marriages, and related poignant tales about AIDS (from the viewpoint of both survivors and those who'd lost partners).

We were by no means the only straight people there, but most likely the only ones on a MysteryDate. Ultimately, the only mystery the panel couldn't solve for us was why so many people feel threatened by homosexuality.

Part 20

Family

"You can please some of the family all of the time and all of the family some of the time, but you can't please all of the family all of the time." Sure, that's not exactly what Abe Lincoln said but it's close enough, especially since this section of the book is all about pleasing "them," your incomparable kin.

We're talkin' big families here. Or, for that matter, little families. Big kids, little kids. Young folks, old folks.

Every individual in *my* family seems to have, er, well-defined individualized interests — and various attention spans when it comes to travel and appetite and almost everything else. What could possibly fit all sizes and shapes? That may still take a few decades to determine. But a homily immediately leaps to mind: If at first you don't succeed, try, try again.

How any given family MysteryDate® is custom-tailored will vary according to *your* personal cravings — not at all different than it is for couples.

You might have your kin-group follow (or accompany) you, the sole person who knows what's up. Or you could tell only the females (except for those charming little girls who couldn't keep a secret if their fashionable frocks depended on it). Or all the males (except for those precocious pre-teen boys who couldn't keep a secret if their nascent testosterone depended on it). Or maybe just the one or two random relatives you do trust to keep their lips locked. If you truly believe the kids can stick to a hush-hush game, you might want to let them in on what's in store but hold off telling their parents.

It's all like sale-shopping in a supermarket or department store's bargain basement: Mix and match.

One guy I know has eight siblings. Each has mastered at least two instruments, so there's always been music at family outings. These almost-post-pandemic days, I know they'd love a break, perhaps a MysteryDate involving *someone else's* concert. In contrast, we know a small family that hates indoor events but adores camping. They'd undoubtedly find a trip to a unique backwoods site thrilling. Other families ride bicycles all over the world, or play golf, tennis, or other sports. Together. Always together. So, hiring a pro that gives lessons might be a treat for them. Or some might enjoy a day trip to almost any athletic event where they *don't* have to cycle.

One good starting place is what might be labeled standard-issue family get-togethers.

Eons ago, my family had a cousin's club that met several times each year to share good food and rambling conversation. Games occupied the toddlers, keeping them in one place and preventing them from playing tag in the living room. Pacifiers kept the infants moderately quiet. As the kids grew up and had kids, and then their kids had kids, the numbers increased exponentially. It got to where I couldn't remember all the surnames, much less the first ones. At that point, I simply stopped counting how many people arrived for the reunion.

But I couldn't stop counting the days — once upon a time early in our relationship — when I planned to drag Nancy on a MysteryDate to a family outing. I didn't expect for a minute that she'd like every person there, but I was sure the event would be entertaining. It was. Relatively speaking, so to speak. That's because clan members, like most folks, liked talking about their own jobs and lives and hobbies, and because attendees ranged from two upwardly mobile, profanity-slinging truck-drivers to a hermit-like researcher who lived in a one-room Brooklyn flat with stacks and stacks of paper containing scribbled notes for a dictionary he was compiling on the etymology of slang words. All Nance had to do was volunteer an open-ended phrase like, "Tell me about your occupation, what you do. It sounds fascinating," and they were off and running.

Because we now live on the West Coast and most of my family still lives in New York state and Georgia, we've sporadically imported them — in ones, twos, threes, and fours. They've visited many times, sleeping on sofas, the floor, or wherever they decided to curl up, and over the years we've schlepped them to a myriad of gripping places. Our grandchildren now range in age from 17 to 36, so that gives us the chance to repeat some places and events.

A sampling of what we've already done includes taking kids and grandkids (and the children of friends and neighbors) to countless museums (to see historical ships, kiddie performances, science exhibits, and wax figurines). We've also been to the usual touristy asks.

On our "been there, done that" list is bowling, bubble festivals, a conservatory of flowers, a fort that features a dramatization of how a cannon is loaded and shot, a horse race at a state fair, indoor (and outdoor) climbing of walls, merry-go-rounds, miniature golf, a planetarium, a playground whose structures are based on what local kids wanted, pro baseball and basketball games, a redwood forest, regular and animal-free circuses, a space center, the top of a mountain, a treasure hunt along the ocean, watching a lunar eclipse from a beach, and water parks. Plus, an indoor concert of a symphony with the musicians playing background music to cartoons, and an outdoor concert of Beatles music in our hometown.

Whew!

We've also involved our families in computer and board games, farms, prepping food, skating, and train trips.

One time, Nance was able to pull off a behind-the-scenes MysteryDate tour for a bunch of family members because she was doing public relations for the zoo. It included some close encounters of the giraffe and koala kind. Our grandchildren loved feeding them, holding or petting them, and asking about four hundred questions. Per critter.

A caution: If *you* go, wear comfortable clothes. Animals tend to drool, lick, shed, and act, well, like animals.

A stimulus package

Family MysteryDates can become irregular or regular changes in routine that stimulate everyday life and strengthen bonds. They can take place at home, at mealtime, or at a specially dreamt up game night.

They can be an impromptu, do-it-yourself version of So *You Think You Can Dance*, or a screechy karaoke free-for-all. They can be a streaming an evening filled with the youngsters teaching the grown-ups new ways to negotiate the latest digital devices or social media.

You might find great fun in such instant dates as or making a video of a family sing-along and screening it on

TikTok, FaceTime, Skype, YouTube, Zoom or some other site that launched just last night.

You also might spring a surprise *during* a regular conversation — doing a magic trick for a child, for instance, right after declaring the interruption a MysteryDate, or flashing some recent snapshots to a grandparent. You could follow up by gifting a relative a digital version of what you've displayed.

In-person sessions work, too (like reading aloud to a group or scheduling an evening in which *everyone* takes turns reading aloud). Or you could:

- Make a snowman or a tree house.
- Scribble hopscotch boxes in chalk on your sidewalk.
- Try doing a family cleanup (maybe with a prize for collecting the biggest dust-bunny).
- Watch a parade.
- Conduct a riddle-athon (making them up as you go along, perhaps with a prize for the worst pun).
- Play catch.
- Take a walk together in part of your hometown — or theirs — where you've never been.
- Listen to music (with each person getting to pick a tune).
- Explore open spaces with your pooch.
- Run, stroll, or swim.
- Stargaze with a telescope.
- Create a game of hide-and-seek.

Not incidentally, the idea of MysteryDates needn't be limited to your generation. You can pass it down. Or up. Nance's daughter, Laura Schifrin, for instance, is now taking her partner, Adam Fox (who's *not* related to my wife), on them. And vice versa.

It also doesn't matter where you live (or visit). In Idaho, for example, you can find more than 80,000 square miles of outdoor recreational prospects (and, if you like, you can easily pick a spot where you're unlikely to bump into too many people — the population of that entire area is only 1.4 million).

It's possible there to rent (or bring your own) all-terrain vehicles or mountain bikes to explore the less-traveled miles of trails and old logging roads, slip back to Old West mentality via a wagon ride, skip along the white-waters, or take off in a hot-air balloon. The state's fly-fishing is legendary, I'm told, and so is the bird and wildlife watching. You also can square dance or walk along a ridge that follows the historical trail taken by Lewis & Clark (c'mon now, you *do* remember them from your high school textbooks, don't you?). And if you're creative while vacationing there you might contemplate inventing a hot-potato game (one starring Mrs. or Mr. Potato Head) or a diversion centering on how many potato skins you can peel in X-number of minutes. After all, most folks do visualize the tuber when they think of Idaho.

No matter what you do, when it comes to family MysteryDates, away or at home, I highly recommend that you remember the ancient acronym affirmation, KISS: keep it simple, stupid. My experience is that the chances for success seem to increase the more minimal an idea is. Clearly, the more people involved, the more complicated it's apt to become.

Don't want to do all the planning yourself? Maybe you can convince another family member to set up a MysteryDate once a year. Or monthly. Or find a place that offers "something for everybody" — such as a traditional amusement park. Bumper cars, go-carts, rollercoasters, and/or midway games can become standard fare for those who don't stop breathing at the thought of dropping a small bundle of cash.

The most extensive? Try Hersheypark in Hershey, Pennsylvania, which contains not only rollercoasters but water slides and chocolate galore. Or Six Flags Magic Mountain in Valencia, California, which boasts 18 coasters. Or Busch Gardens in Tampa, Florida, which, in addition to the rides (including the country's tallest freestanding drop tower), offers 2,700 zoo animals that may stare back at you. And even though there's always the stalwart DisneyLand in Anaheim and Disney World in Lake Buena Vista, Florida, to visit, don't forget to check out that small, low-tech park near you or some touring carnivals that have exciting rides. They undoubtedly cost a lot less than the nationally known entities.

But whatever you opt for, the keys to family happiness — as in many other situation — probably depend on two rules of thumb: Be flexible. Bring along a sense of humor (and perhaps some chocolate chip cookies.)

Cruising — and a bruising

How to find or keep the sizzle in a relationship has been the underlying theme of this book, so, it figures, the concept usually applies to families as well. Not only do parents of toddlers have a kaleidoscopic array of choices in front of their noses, so do grandparents.

My highly creative granddaughter never seemed to care much whether I took her to a highly structured party or an almost barren park because she'd inevitably devise her own good time. But I vividly recall, in contrast, a "Lollipopalooza" MysteryDate that Nance calculated was perfect for her — an event featuring four children's performers and a band. Replete with a pocketful of lollipops for her to lick. The rest of the young, gleefully noisy audience sang along, clapped, tapped, and danced with the three of us joining in and adding to the programmed-down-to-the-minute ruckus.

For those who haven't heard, Lake Tahoe is a winter wonderland for gamblers, skiers, snowshoers, and sportsmen. So, it provided a perfect backdrop for Nance to take the grandkid and her mom on an estrogen-based family MysteryDate road trip where they could introduce the then-three-year-old to snow. Another highlight came in the form of Abraham, a huge horse that dutifully pulled them in an old-fashioned sled as "Jingle Bells" kept playing, just long enough for a toddler's attention span.

Yet another time, in the summer, I dragged my entire family on a MysteryDate to a water park. It was pure pleasure sneaking into their suitcases to ferret out bathing suits without anyone being the wiser.

I've also surfed the net with the grandkids, sung, toyed with Nance's puppets and self-made rhythm instruments, and trumped-up stories (many of them involving a crocodile family I'd invented). Why not morph similar ideas into your own private fantasy trips?

Universal satisfaction from a MysteryDate that includes older youngsters, especially teens, can be a bit more difficult to accomplish. Ergo, if you can afford it (financially and emotionally), consider a cruise that offers something for all ages.

For my then-20-year-old grandson, Drew Brown, an adventure to the Mexican Riviera turned into cruising of a different kind: trolling for girls. All was going well until he decided to do a show-off backflip for a small circle of them. Owww! He landed on his tailbone and was too sore the next day to take part in another activity he'd been coveting, a ping-pong tournament. But he ultimately found, during the seven-day outing, a bunch of activities that suited him perfectly. And enough snack foods (pizza, hot dogs, and burgers, naturally) to stuff his belly while the rest of us picked gloriously from several deliciously excessive buffets.

Periodically, he and I would groan almost in unison: "Oh My God, I overate."

Part 21

Parades, festivals

With or without 76 trombones, parades are ubiquitous. But truth be told, the odds are you can't cite off the top of your head how many of them *your* community puts on each year.

Maybe, however, you'd prefer to make your MysteryDate® one in a million. The Macy's Thanksgiving event in Manhattan can give you that opportunity. It forces more than 999,999 to scramble each year for an in-person, up-front glimpse while 45 million or so settle for being couch potatoes and watch it on TV.

If you can't get enough of jammed streets, you can add to your calendar the Tournament of Roses Parade on New Year's Day in Pasadena — or the mid-July Cornucopia Days Grand Parade in Kent, Washington, where its Lions Club sponsors might be upset that you've never heard of it.

Often electrifying are gay-pride marches that take place in cities such as Atlanta, Boston, Chicago, Dallas, Honolulu, New Hope, Orlando, Paris, Phoenix, San Francisco, Syracuse, and Watsonville — as well as communities in Brazil, Canada, Holland, Israel, and Thailand. Expect public shows of affection (and a public airing of body parts not usually displayed).

African American pride also gets a big spotlight annually — particularly in Atlanta, when the Black History Month Parade blends heritage and culture.

A less serious-minded effort regularly occurs in another community — in Enterprise, Arkansas, to be exact, site of what's termed The World's Shortest St. Patrick's Day Parade. One man or woman of Irish descent (out of the 23,000 who live there) makes up the entire show — marching back and forth across a 98-foot bridge. He or she totes a pot of gold and recites limericks while strolling. Grand marshals, who serve in absentia, are picked by essays that include excuses why, if selected, they *won't* attend.

Back in San Francisco, both the yearly Chinese New Year parade and a spectacle in Japantown almost *demand* attention and attendance. You might think that since both cultures are Asian-oriented, there'd be a common denominator. Wrong! The Chinese event is crammed with colorful dragons, masks, costumes, dancing, and 100 units marching down the street for hours. Not to mention the excitement of ear-shattering noise, including what seems like never-ending firecrackers. Similarly, the Japanese event showcases taiko drummers who can, indeed, simulate thunder, although that's the lone loud part of the city's Cherry Blossom Festival. Mostly, classical and folk dancers quietly float through flower-laden streets alongside martial artists and 100 men who tote a portable Shinto shrine 4-1/2 blocks from the top of a hill.

Wannabe MysteryDaters who double as agoraphobics needn't — rather than venture outside — do more than flip on TVs to catch those events.

Parading isn't limited to either the outdoors *or* TV, of course: Sightseeing's also available on fashionable runways. Professional and amateur pageants across America march Miss, Ms., or Mr. Fill-in-the-Blank hopefuls down those narrow pathways. And that counts only the adults. There are hundreds of children's events (both standard and "glitz" versions). Even parades of "beautiful babies."

Vast numbers of U.S. high schools stage pageants year after year as well.

But perhaps you'd rather see an array of sea creatures. Well, Disney World provides it: the Electrical Water Pageant in Orlando.

Not to your liking? Why not a do-it-yourself MysteryDate then: a family history cavalcade, let's say (your own parade of digitized or albumized photos)? And although a straightforward approach normally is advisable, satire is another possibility. Either way, you could insert a song or two believed to be family favorites, or create a sing-along (a cappella or a group hum-athon).

Whatever's meaningful to *you* should work, anything from "M-i-c-k-e-y-M-o-u-s-e" to "Battle Hymn of the Republic."

Plunge-ing ahead

The annual small-town parade in Fairfax, California, is quintessentially funky, frivolous, and funny. And only several blocks long.

But our midlife friends went all-out to create the most captivating bride-and-groom float local parade-viewers had ever seen.

He, sporting tux jacket, jeans, and sneakers, and she, in a theatrical, ruffled vintage gown with a train that seemed to go on for a block (and required a small army of friends to keep from dragging on the street), were perched on a high chariot "bejeweled" with a huge makeshift ring topped by an equally huge plastic diamond that reflected the sun. His parents, a little behind them, were pulled in something that looked like a miniature tugboat. In front were four female gal-pals in polka-dotted strapless vintage gowns singing, "Going to the Chapel" — in what they fruitlessly hoped would be four-part harmony.

Nancy initially thought we were just going to watch the annual parade, but I had something else in mind — a MysteryDate, of course. I'd secretly stashed our garb in our car trunk. When we parked, I whisked it out. "Wear this," I said, struggling with a four-foot bear costume that had been part of her act as a children's performer years ago. "And carry this, please." I handed her an oversized wedding ring I'd made from cardboard. "OK," she groaned and grinned. "I get it. I'm the 'ring bear-er.' But what are *you* going to be?"

I said nothing but removed my shirt, pulled one of her nightgowns over my head, covering my Bermuda shorts, and picked up a bouquet of extremely wilted flowers (carefully plucked from our back yard). With hairy legs sticking out, and with lacey gloves and size-14 sandaled feet accessorizing my wedding outfit, I'd become a slightly bizarre, instant bearded flower girl.

The crowd loved "the look." They cheered us both — and the entire wedding party, in fact.

Our friends — Michael Rosenberg and Marleen Roggow — did get married for real later that day, as planned months before. In regular wedding outfits. In a beautiful garden setting. We didn't wear the bear, the cardboard ring, or the nightie to that ceremony. We had no wilted flowers. But we have treasured the memory of both mock wedding and the real thing.

Another year, Nance and I witnessed our longtime plumber, Bobby Sandler — who was tugged in an antique bathtub, leading his minions — pull off a pseudo-military routine with a hefty contingent of helpers dressed in coveralls and tall rubber boots. Military music blasted from a tape recorder as the group marched in tight formation, stopping periodically to simulate an Army drill team. Plungers replaced rifles, though. Resting on shoulders. Twirling over biceps. Flying end-over-end above the marchers. Fabulous.

But I did notice that they weren't truly at the top of their professional game: They failed to check out the street sewers.

Scarecrows and space cadets

Most festivals fit into one classification: Mob scenes with thousands of eyewitnesses and three or four times as many smiles. Depending on where your home is, you probably won't have to travel far to find one. And if you happen to be visiting...

The MadFest Juggling Festival, which has been drawing large audiences for close to half a century, would allow you to discover the offspring of a student jugglers' club that specializes in unicyling and "other related object manipulation, balance [and] performance skills" at the University of Wisconsin. Its website is clear: "We're just a bunch of folks who like to get together and throw things."

Much more grounded, literally, is the Scarecrow Festival in Wanatah, Indiana, with a kiddie-pedal tractor pull, duck raffle, and it figures, scarecrow-sculpting. Its many prizes include one for the soybean stalk with the most pods. Banned are alcohol, smoking, bikes, lasers, weapons, and silly string.

Variety, for MysteryDate seekers, is the operative word:
- The National Peanut Festival in Dothan, Alabama, crowns a new Little Miss Peanut each year.
- For those who can't get enough flora, there's the Daffodil Festival, which kicks off the tourist season on Chincoteague Island, on the eastern shore of Virginia.
- The Vermont Quilt Festival, in Essex Junction, has grown, much like many a patchwork-quilt, from petite (starting with a few dedicated historians and quilters) to semi-gigantic.
- The unique Frog Leg Festival in 3,000-population Fellsmere, Florida, is held in January (when, if you're not hot for the skinny extremities, you can chomp on gator tails instead).
- In Pittsburgh, a three-day pickle festival in July, with a 35-foot-high pickle balloon as its "Picklesburgh" centerpiece, claims to supply a "dill-icious time."
- Providing a sharp contrast is Roswell, New Mexico, where, at its UFO Festival, also in July, solemn researchers, film buffs, and probably a few space cadets gather to explore "ufology." An Alien Idol is celebrated, and costumed True Believers (including some laying no claim to ever having been abducted) gaily gain access.
- For those seeking more easily identified moving objects, Trenary, Michigan, proudly boasts an annual Outhouse Classic each February, a downhill race starring — you guessed it — porta-potties.

Have a particularly strong stomach? Then you can test the annual testicle festival in sundry Missouri towns where the prime attraction is fried turkey gonads. Unusual? Yup, but not the *most* unusual item my research turned up. That designation, I'd venture to say, belonged to a previously annual event in Telluride, Colorado, that never tried to compete with any others — the mid-summer Nothing Festival, where "not much happened," sometimes not even any performers. It promised no crowds and no traffic, and organizers pledged "sunrises and sunsets as normal" and that "gravity will continue to be in effect." Its website had flaunted a sign that proclaimed, "Thank you for not participating."

Since it isn't happening anymore, obviously *nothing* prevailed.

In a similar vein, a house in my San Anselmo hometown still has this playful sign on its gate: "On this site in 1782, nothing historical happened."

Part 22

Book readings

Johannes Gutenberg, the father of printing, could never have conceived of Kindle, e-books, iPads, iPhones, audio books, and gazillion new apps that seem to emerge by the hour.

Nor could he have conceived of author readings, which occasionally have less to do with text than performance mode and which became pre- and post-pandemic standing-room-only events at both independents and the last major U.S chain-bookstore standing, Barnes & Noble — as well as in libraries.

Those readings draw packs of book-buyers, aficionados, and folks who merely want autographs, photos, a handshake, or an up-close-and-personal glimpse of a celebrity (at the same time Amazon is working up a corporate sweat trying to kill off most brick-and-mortar storefronts).

For MysteryDate® addicts, or wannabes, the in-person talks (some mega-stores can schedule a couple a day) can be a marvelous way to plan a free or cheap, entertaining date. And since author appearances usually coincide with interviews on local radio and TV stations, listening to or viewing such a conversation together at home can also be turned into an intriguing date. Hosts, by the way, may or may not have a clue what's between the covers (though they're usually aware, in their never-ending quest for ratings, who's between every author's sheets).

Either way, all you need up-front is familiarity with your partner's tastes (at least knowledge of whether she or he leans toward the esoteric or scientific, sci-fi or mystery, trashy best-sellers or luminously literary, gravitas-laden or comic).

Oh, yeah, here's another helpful hint: It's even better if you and your partner are — you saw it coming, didn't you? — on the same page.

Doing it 'by the book'

I must admit being elated at a recent MysteryDate I managed to pull off *after* Nancy had originally scheduled it. Lemme explain.

When something unexpected came up (our desire to meet with a newbie friend, actually), my wife canceled her plan to hear comic Paula Poundstone at our favorite local indie bookseller. Saddened a bit, Nance couldn't help telling me what we'd be missing. So, a short time later, when our friend suddenly needed to cancel, my brain went into fifth gear. Why shouldn't I take my wife to see Poundstone on a Nance-won't-guess-it-in-a-million-years MysteryDate. I did, and we both laughed aloud for more than an hour as the NPR *Wait Wait...Don't Tell Me* panelist and stand-up dealt with "the down and dirty true story of raising three children" *and* the 14 cats she adopted.

I wouldn't be letting the cat out of the time-honored bag, incidentally, to tell you that Nance and I have intermittently been swapping bookshop MysteryDates for years.

Have I mentioned, by the way, that I'm a film buff as well as book shop browser? Sometimes I think I've seen every "A" movie ever made (as well as most "B" flicks, more than a few "C" choices and, I confess, a handful from the "Z" worst-ever lists) because I started viewing films as soon as I could sit up without help (back, I think, when Walt Disney came out with his original *Snow White and the Seven Dwarfs*). I occasionally wonder if my mom looked at cinema when I was in utero.

I'll watch *any* genre, a fetish incomprehensible to Nance (who's only addicted to music and reading). So, it shouldn't have surprised me one iota that she'd programmed a MysteryDate to hear my then film guru, Roger Ebert, the guy who invented the "thumbs up" gimmick. He was still traveling the bookstore circuit before thyroid cancer robbed him of his voice and his life. Ebert's books (including the encyclopedic composites of his lifetime of film reviews), his syndicated newspaper column, and his TV programs had long become my virtual combo Bible for all things cinematic — with material by A.O. Scott of *The New York Times* running a close second.

Nance was confident I wouldn't know about Ebert's appearance because she'd specifically hidden the bookstore's extensive newsletter (still surprising, she noted later, because "you immediately read everything in sight, including milk cartons and the fine print of legal documents"). At any rate, we lucked out and found seats (so many people were willing to stand for the critic's informal talk, it had to be simulcast to an overflow crowd outdoors). Ebert, as I might have been guessed, was warm, funny, engrossing, and informative. And he graciously answered question after question. "That was fantabulous," I exclaimed afterward, giving Nance's MysteryDate initiative a thumbs-up.

I gave the same sign after a reading by Letty Cottin Pogrebin, feminist journalist, and founding editor of Ms. Magazine and the author of volumes relating to women in business and non-sexist child-rearing. A lifelong newspaperman who was then editing a local weekly, I had assigned a feature story on her to a reporter several months before. It figured, then, that once Nance learned Pogrebin was coming, she'd set up the MysteryDate, again sneakily snatching a paper listing about the upcoming event so I wouldn't catch on. What ultimately happened? The writer effortlessly charmed our collective socks off. While being erudite.

Francis Bacon once claimed that "some books are to be tasted, others to be swallowed, and some few to be chewed and digested." We agree with each part of that quote. And we've repeatedly found that in-person words of authors can provide especially tantalizing food for thought, food for the soul, food for the funny-bone.

One book at a time. Or as Annie Lamott winningly wrote, "bird by bird."

Paging Mr. and Ms. MysteryDate

Dozens of unread books lie around our home in small piles labeled (in our minds-eyes, anyway) "gifts from friends," "gifts I'd like to give to friends," "books I want to re-read," and "books I don't know what to do with but just can't give away." Any and all, of course, can lead to a MysteryDate.

Your stacks can be as meaningful. How about, for instance, setting up a session where you and your partner, Mr. and Ms. MysteryDate, go through your heaps and just make some decisions? Or wrap and give those presents to friends (for no special occasion, preferably)? Or visit a charity thrift shop with armloads? Or plan a date with friends who bring their own orphaned volumes and set up a trading party? If none of those notions work for you in the moment, consider them next month. Or next year.

Your local public library (or even a private one where you need special permission to enter) can also be a primo place for a MysteryDate. Just stroll in and browse. Look at categories you've never thought much about. Then take out an audiobook or antiquated CD you'd both like to hear while *en route* to wherever.

Libraries not only have author readings but book and poetry groups you can enjoy jointly. And children's reading clubs (sometimes with prizes) and performances. All usually fee-less.

You could also check out nearby yard or garage sales, or Friends of the Library bargain days, to select tomes you can read together. You could even start a book group with friends and use the first meeting as the venue for a MysteryDate.

Are you both writers, or one of you a scribe and the other a researcher? If so, how about beginning a joint project with your partner — like a book outlining your lives together (intended for your eyes only, or those of relatives)? That's not only possible but is comparatively easy to publish these days as a do-it-yourselfer. You could also create a volume that contains short profiles of each of those relatives. It could be totally positive (ergo unrealistic) or snarky (realistic perhaps but inappropriate to show anybody else).

How about creating a book for kids together? I didn't create a MysteryDate around it because I published it during the pandemic, but I'm sure that under other circumstances I could have concocted a date based on *Grampy and His Fairyzona Playmates*, a book for children I co-wrote with my then-8-year-old granddaughter.

Other ideas? Why not create book covers for the mounds of papers you intend to keep until death do you part — or, possibly, set up a MysteryDate to make them as historic gifts to heirs. Materials might include only a plain brown-paper bag and some colored tape. For the truly crafty, a bookend-making scheme might work. Just search around your home or thrift store for unusual objects you can use (matching ones would make a set, of course, but then, come to think of it, so might mismatched items). The range can be from scrap wood to antique shoe molds.

One of our pals recently presented us with personalized bookmarks she made by sewing odd buttons to lengths of ribbon in coordinated colors. It inspired us to ponder how we could make some out of scraps of this 'n' that we've neither used nor tossed out.

Believe you're too organized to have any "junk" around? Rubbish!

Images and imagination

Filmmakers frequently find inspiration in best-selling books, figuring there's a built-in audience. They may have unknowingly built in a potential MysteryDate as well.

The thriller trilogy by Swedish author Stieg Larsson, for example, caused a major sensation a while back and inspired a trio of Swedish films (*The Girl with the Dragon Tattoo*, *The Girl Who Played with Fire*, and *The Girl Who Kicked the Hornet's Nest*). And, as naturally as lava flows downhill, a Hollywood offshoot — much less mesmerizing — followed. If you'd read any of the three, you might have taken your partner on a MysteryDate to see the movie adaptation. Had you not read the books, you could have reversed the process — seen the films first and then checked out the novels from the library later. You could also have done it with another couple as a double date.

Need more possibilities? Try linking your insights with those of your favorite author and then discussing new ideas, philosophies, or political views. Or follow the imaginative idea of a well-heeled friend who years ago adopted our MysteryDate concept. On her partner's 60th birthday, she took her to a local shop and gave her "an hour — one minute for each birthday" to select as many books as she wanted.

Seventy-three books later...

Part 23

Discoveries

Don't just sit there. Don't just stand there. Do something. You may at times be unsure what you'll discover, or what'll happen, on a MysteryDate®. But if you stay at home mentally struggling to escape *whatever* rut you've slipped into, you'll *never* find out.

Here's a way to break the redundancy and find unexpected, fabulous delights: Ask yourself, "What haven't we done that I think we'd both like?" From there, things can unfold organically.

A few "staycations" could potentially not only save you Big Bucks but bring on some fever-pitched euphoria at the same time. Leave the responsibilities of your cell (your phone, hopefully, not jail) and to-do lists behind. Do, however, print out a digital map of where you live and draw a circle showing areas within an hour's drive — or one tank of high-priced gas if you prefer. Or, maybe even easier, have Waze or some other computer app list nearby places you might enjoy. A tiny amount of your own online research usually can pinpoint what's out there that you're not familiar with or haven't given a first thought, much less a second. Too lazy to do the research yourself? Pick the brains of the staff at your community's Chamber of Commerce or your community's chief librarian.

For some couples there may be nothing better than arriving, parking, and wandering around somewhere unfamiliar at their own sloth-like pace (Nancy and I call it "becoming meanderthals"). Normally, if somebody told me to "get lost," I'd perceive the suggestion as an insult; my wife and I have learned, though, to love losing our way in strange places we stumble onto (or into), mainly because we so often locate semi-precious trinkets and new sights (or insights), not to mention fascinating locals who tout us onto even more.

At home, it's relatively easy for quickie brainstorming sessions to morph into hands-on, do-it-yourself events — to simultaneously create short- or long-lived keepsakes while experiencing MysteryDates. It doesn't matter if either or neither of you have any talent, so long as you make an ersatz advance-pact, pinky-swearing, to appreciate the probably flawed end-product.

The first step? Choose from among pounds of recycled odds-and-ends that you've collected specifically for this purpose: candy-bar wrappers, chipped jars, clothespins, computer innards, egg cartons, empty film canisters, miscellaneous items from nature like leaves or pine cones or twigs, old game parts, old greeting cards, paper, paperclips, pieces of broken jewelry, Styrofoam, tops of soda bottles, vinyl records. In short, pretty much anything you can find. Add a glue gun or sparkles or spray paint, followed by a tincture of time, and, yes, that requisite pinch of imagination. The result? Anybody's guess.

You could come up with a tangible but indescribable thingie to be carefully stationed indoors or out as idiosyncratic statuary. Or maybe a centerpiece. Or a holiday decoration. Birdhouse? Doll? Flowerpot? Gargoyle, mask, or puppet? Hat? Montage or finger-painting? Rattle? Vase?

You might build an entire party around the idea, even tossing in an element of creative storytelling that invents a tale about Creation. You might, in fact, build a permanent home for your concoction to live in, and maybe even name it (we put together a life-sized, 3D sculpture out of multi-colored balls of yarn and then had the nerve to give the resultant wall-hanging the moniker *Clive Cojones*).

You clearly can do whatever you desire with your partner alone. Or you can have your kids, or the enemies you want to hold close, or those nosy new neighbors join in.

To get over any nervousness that might linger about lack of ability, why not pretend you're a kindergarten teacher? Or a kindergartner.

Maybe scraps of food make better supplies in your mind than scraps of would-be art. To cook up a tasty MysteryDate cake, start with a solo trek to a local market and then spread the ingredients in front of your partner. Or don't even bother purchasing new goodies. Forage in the refrigerator and pantry to find leftover or long neglected foodstuffs that make both of you tingle. Start chopping and sautéing and what have you got? Ratatouille. Salad. Soup. An unknown, unnamed, never-before-constructed concoction.

If that sort of exercise in discovery isn't your cup of designer tea, try a MysteryDate cooking class with your partner. All levels and kinds are yours for the taking — from vegetarian to meat-laden Italian, from expansive Thai or Cambodian to quickie fast-food greaseburgers. If don't want to be limited by the rigidity of a class, watch a TV cooking show in tandem and dish up a meal yourselves.

Here's a handful of other discovery-date ideas:
- THE SKY'S THE LIMIT. Check online or your newspaper or local planetarium to determine when the next meteor shower will happen. Rent or buy an inexpensive telescope, or just go outside at the designated hour and watch beyond the clouds. It can be awesome. And romantic.
- CLASS ACTIONS. Pick your poison, as they say, and enroll in a seminar. Many local institutions and rec departments provide sundry roads to no-charge, introductory pupildom. Near us, for instance, is a place that offers a Capoeira class, a combo Brazilian discipline for singing, dancing, and self-defense.
- TRIVIAL PURSUIT. Nance pulled off one of those game-night MysteryDates in a local pub and, later, another in a private home. Both times we chuckled a lot as we taunted and teased our brains (even though, in the first instance, taunting our stomach on English bangers turned out not to be our smartest choice ever). And I've turned the tables, so to speak, by taking her in a lower-brow direction to a Bingo night (where she handily proceeded to out-dab me).
- INNER PURSUIT. Want to put what yellowed bumper stickers playfully call "inner peas" on your plate? Try walking a labyrinth. I discovered a makeshift one on top of a hill in Marin County built by hikers. Rather find out what cards reveal? A Tarot reading can for sure be the basis of an unusual MysteryDate. And if that's not your Three Cups of Tea, what about an astrological session? Where's your sun sign? What's your ruling planet? Do you have more earth signs than your partner? Do I have the lingo wrong,

and what in heaven's name does any of that mean anyway?

Sand-in-the-shoes spectators

Does a fad that's lasted three decades count as contemporary, classic, or historic? I'd say the label makes no-never-mind if what's being experienced is entertaining. Like sandcastle-building.

Such organized beach events take place regularly in Galveston, New York, San Diego, Siesta Key in Florida, and Washington. But we, as you may have guessed, did our MysteryDate in what some wags still call Baghdad by the Bay. As liberal, liberated sand-in-the-shoes spectators, not strict constructionists.

For nearly 30 years, teams of architects, contractors, designers, school kids, and plain ole sand-lovers have competed, patted, and shoveled to raise money for hands-on art-and-architecture programs in San Francisco Bay Area schools through an agency named Leap. But anyone can, for free, check out the sand-made antique cars, giant octopuses and frogs, guitar-playing dragons, historical and movie characters, sleeping giants, slinky mermaids, and ten-foot sea turtles that evolve out of granules over four hours. Not to mention elaborate castles, naturally.

In the end, also naturally, it's the sands of time that triumph as ocean waves gently caress and then pulverize the sculptures.

Our own sandy memories don't ever wash away, though. Nor do our desires to *repeat* a date — the following day, the next month, years later — that went especially well. Or twist 'em just a little bit. I've deemed those "flip-flops" but also occasionally call them "turnabouts" (as in "turnabout is fair play"). Or, when I insist on puntificating, "getting our redux in a row." Others might label such events copycats, but the labels don't really matter. What it boils down to is this: If I've successfully arranged a date with Nance as my in-the-dark companion, she may replicate it in the future. Or vice versa. But reasonable facsimiles, spin-offs, and tangents are quite acceptable.

For example, if I've taken her to a conservatory of flowers, that might trigger her to plan a follow-up date in which we plant foliage together. Or prepare a dinner with edible flora. If she's scheduled a recycling afternoon in which we grab "a pile of crap" from our home and take it to a thrift shop or donation center (or, if all else fails, the dump), I might create a date a week later in which we take old photos we can't identify and make a Braque-like montage out of cut-outs.

The only limit, once again, is our ingenuity, inspiration, and inventiveness — on the shoulders, so to speak, of other creatives.

Cackle, giggle, and titter

Comedy, or humor, it's been said (especially by defensive comics who've bombed), is in the eye of the beholder (or on the tongue of the comic). So, let's start with the presumption that you know what makes your partner laugh. From there, it should be effortless — just set up a MysteryDate and watch your other's face light up.

In Japan, many women giggle with eyes cast downward while covering their mouths; in the USA, we cackle, chortle, giggle, guffaw. laugh, snicker, or titter. Boisterously. You don't have to leave home to make one or t'other occur, though. You can create events that incorporate comedy in your apartment, complex, estate, house, or man- or woman-cave (with small or not-so-small groups of living, breathing bipeds).

In search of a smile, you might:
- Write limericks on whatever topic you select — or about each other (as long as neither of you has thin skin).
- Create funny games or humorous songs.
- Have friends bring their favorite jokes on 3x5 cards and act them out. Or whip up badly drawn pictures of each other and tell the group why you distorted what.
- Laugh at classic cartoons like *The Far Side.*

You also can set up a MysteryDate that involves reading rib-tickling writing (by David Sedaris, Fran Lebowitz, or Dr. Seuss, perhaps) to your partner or pal. If you're hell-bent on getting away from home, you could attend a Los Angeles sitcom taping and compete with its laugh track. Lazier folk might discover that movie theaters and film festivals in their small communities feature the identical comedians as in even more citizen-cramped Mumbai.

Streaming is, of course, the more up to date, more-frequent option. If you happen to be exhausted, just stay in bed, download a comedy flick, and fashion a private, custom-fitted Night on the Couch. Or, for that matter, a Week on the Couch.

Years ago, when Nance was healing from breast cancer surgery, radiation, and chemotherapy, we rented almost every comedy film known to womankind. It helped pass the time for months — and cheered up both of us. Although, truthfully, no MysteryDates were involved, it did make us recognize how valuable laughing is. And to some degree,

Nance chuckled herself well for more than a quarter of a century.

In our extended backyard, San Francisco, the annual "Comedy Day" in Golden Gate Park long ago became one of our faves after I discovered the event via a press release. When I parked the first time near what's since been renamed Robin Williams Meadow, Nance figured out *where* we were going because she spotted hundreds of people walking in the same direction as we, schlepping beach chairs and food. The *what* came seconds later. Mingling backstage at an event that's been a free summer tradition since 1975 were almost 40 comics waiting for their five-minute sets, representing nearly every ethnicity, disability, philosophy, religion, sexual orientation, and weight. More than 600 comics have performed there for more than half a million people over the years.

We consider ourselves extremely lucky to have seen (many of them multiple times), as well as Williams, a virtual Who's Who of Funny: Diane Amos, Dana Carvey, Margaret Cho, Billy Crystal, Ellen DeGeneres, Will Durst, Janeane Garofalo, Whoopie Goldberg, Bobcat Goldthwait, George Lopez, Don Novello, Patton Oswalt, Pat Paulson, Kevin Pollak, Paula Poundstone, Greg Proops, Bob Saget, Rob Schneider, Gary Shandling, and Bobby Slayton.

Every year the event draws a gaggle of gigglers toting, in addition to bubbles, dogs, cameras, iPhones, kids, layers of clothing, nosh and drinks, political handouts, and *The N.Y. Times* (and a lot less elitist reading material), boxes of every size and shape with unidentifiable contents. Snack booths are stocked with allegedly healthy packages (and, as you'd expect, with decidedly unhealthy, sugary stuff). The audience, regularly about 20,000 strong, includes folks wearing glitter or Kiss-type makeup, people decked out in mock formal wear, a handful sporting only thongs, many others in tatters. And women with Rapunzel-like blonde hair and pastel Manolo shoes. Not to mention some barefoot boys with buttock cheeks of tan.

Not incidentally, porta-potties are lined up like azure sentinels, a sanctuary for those who might leak a bit because some of the comedians are *that* funny.

Part 24

Themes

My wife and I are proof you don't need to excel at something to find a triumphant diversion or to plan a MysteryDate® around an activity at which we peak at middling.

Nancy, to cite only one instance, insists she's not a great dancer and is positive she'd never make a good candidate on a TV dance show. "I'm slightly awkward, not exceptionally graceful, and fresh out of skin-tight, skimpy, glittery miniskirts," she says. "But I love to dance anyway. Besides, as George Gershwin put it, 'I Got Rhythm.'"

Nance learned to "follow properly" when she was 13, shortly after her parents enrolled her in ballroom dancing classes in Detroit. As a result, she still knows steps to the cha-cha, fox trot, jitterbug. rhumba, and samba. The fact that missing from her list are the Cannibal, the Renegade, the Wap, and a galaxy of TikTok viral crazes that last about two minutes should reveal how she hasn't quite kept up with trendy moves that may pass their sell-by dates by the time this book makes it into your local library.

She enjoys dancing anyway, in spite of — or because of — my not being a whole lot better at it than she (and, just to be perfectly clear, I don't have a drawer filled with skin-tight, skimpy garments either).

With some irregularity we still take on opportunities to box-step our way to pleasure. You, in contrast, can easily expand that concept and sharpen dancing dates to your taste, ability, age, and interest — perhaps even do the Cannibal, Renegade, Wap, or whatever. And there's definitely no rule that confines anybody to a ballroom.

Still, our favorite dance date was a themed evening my wife planned with disparate elements. First in the sequence of events, she found out that a Hyatt had "tea dancing" every Friday, which consisted of cocktail-hour ballroom dancing to a big band that played old-fashioned, partner-touching music. Participants consisted of locals, tourists, and business travelers, in everything from ragged jeans to pristine formal wear. Among them were young turks barely old enough to shave or drink (boasting about steps they'd learned only days before) and a woman in her 80s whirling and twirling and flaunting her crinolines and undergarments.

For stage two, Nance had purchased tickets to the Joffrey Ballet, and we marveled at the performers' ability to move their lithe bodies in unpredictable and sensuous ways. A late dinner at a Moroccan restaurant, where we ate with our hands while some plump but sexy ladies did their belly dancing thing, sublimely ended our evening.

And because we'd both admittedly relished the entire date, she decided to push her luck a few weeks later: "Here's your chance to be Fred Astaire," she told me as we entered the dance studio for a MysteryDate-style group lesson. Truth be told, neither of us was transformed into Astaire, Gene Kelly, or Ginger Rogers, or even Lady Gaga, then or ever. But we settled for not being the clumsiest couple there. "What *are* our goals?" I'd asked in all sincerity up front. "To keep off each other's feet," she'd answered. And that we managed to do. Mostly.

The joys of dancing, as either spectator or participant sport, can be found almost anywhere. Case in point? Shreveport, Louisiana, where the cowpoke lifestyle merges with the Creole/Cajun, where a spicy crawfish can share a dish with a mammoth Texas T-bone. In that city of 200,000, it's easy as sweet potato pecan pie to find a musical emporium (from bluegrass to hip-hop to jazz) and, with it, dancing.

MysteryDates are also possible at Shreveport golf or country-club dance nights, at the New Year's Eve masquerade ball, at outdoor and indoor festivals that draw hundreds of thousands of visitors, via classes at the Christian Dance Center (in ballet, modern, or tap), through performances of the Louisiana Dance Foundation, by studying African American influences in dance during Black History or any other month, or learning in St. Paul's Episcopal classes or at the more formal dances at the School of the Performing Arts of Louisiana Tech.

Outsiders can test local favorites such as the ballet-oriented pas de deux, the pogo, the sashay, two-step, the "worm," or the Zydeco.

You can, of course, even take dance lessons at home or at a friend's, online!

Yes, it may be best to have some approximate idea of what you're doing on the dance floor (or your kitchen tiles), but those who don't — those with the proverbial two left feet — can have fun anyway.

Fun, indeed, can be found in the most unexpected places. "How'd you like to wear a tutu today?" Nance asked me as we headed out. I scowled in disbelief, but that expression changed to a grin as we entered the event, which I'd heard about but had never attended. And I was game enough to alternate in the silliness with her — each of us sharing the one lone pink tutu we rented on the spot — marching, pirouetting, and waltzing along with the many disparate eventgoers.

The "Dance-along Nutcracker" was invented a little over 30 years ago. Just because they could, I suspect. First performed by the San Francisco Lesbian/Gay Freedom Band, it quickly evolved into a tradition and the most offbeat holiday event in a city famous for offbeat events (holiday-based and otherwise). The core of it, as might be expected, is Tchaikovsky's *Nutcracker Suite*, but its heart and soul is the zany costuming and participation of the crowd. All genders. All ages. All off the wall.

Every year the music is performed differently in San Francisco. You might attend a bizarre vaudeville performance, or one combining elements of *A Christmas Carol* with an arranger's unique twist. But audience antics consistently are the show's highlight.

Dozens of two- and three-year-olds, as well as their dads, moms, and grandparents, put tutus over their street clothes. Some folks come in homemade regalia appropriately accessorized with glitter, tiaras, and wands.

And yes, it's all sooooooooo San Francisco.

A smooth start, but...

Oops!

A key segment of a "Bob" theme-date that took a lot of my advance coordinating was thwarted in an instant or three by a mega-jammed city.

Leg One hornswoggled me by going off perfectly. Smoothly.

As I approached a street fair, a hidden apparatus sloshed around in my trunk: I extracted the small tub filled with water, pointed to the fruit that had sunk to the bottom, and decreed, "We're going to start by bobbing for apples." Nance followed my directions — with a slightly puzzled look on her face. I followed, but my face sported a grin from ear to ear (because I *believed* I knew what was coming).

When lunchtime rolled around after we'd visited a few booths, we had no trouble taking off, but I quickly found that no parking was available near the restaurant at which I'd intended dining. No problem, I thought, "On to my second choice." Minutes later, same story: No open spaces, nobody leaving. Option three extended my frustration. Ergo, I conceded victory to the evil gods of parking meters and admitted to Nance that I'd been seeking a spot near any of the only three eateries in the city with "Bob" in its title.

Fast approaching starvation instead of a parking slot, I decided to settle for the first restaurant with a curbside vacancy that could accommodate my vehicle (I no longer gave a hoot if the joint had Jiminy Cricket in its title and served only beanies and weenies for toddlers). The food — we eventually agreed — was "edible," no worse than a C-minus. With service and ambiance that hovered at lackluster.

Having lived through "near misses" before, Nance grinned and bore it, as did I — except that I burst out in song, in fake lounge-lizard style and only a little off-key, warbling a few pre-planned bars from an oldie that dated back to Al Jolson:

> "I'm just a kid again,
> "Doin' what I did again,
> "Singin' a song,
> "When the red, red robin
> "Comes bob, bob, bobbin' along."

I was so outlandishly bad that my wife couldn't help but smile with me — even as her eyes rolled.

The final part of the date rapidly removed any negative residue. We were enthralled by a concert by The Bobs, three guys and a gal (none of whom were named Bob incidentally) who bemused us with a cappella music, quirky comedy, and a variety of hair colors and styles.

Who you callin' a dummy?

One major theme in our lives has been to try things we haven't done before. Risky? Only a tad. Sure, we're often *unsure* what's next. But the resultant experiences are often exciting. Witness the couples' improvisational theater-game session Nance took me to as MysteryDate.

"Okay," began the instructor, "one half of each couple sits in a chair while your partner stands in back. Everyone who's standing, start talking about anything you want, and the one who's seated, move your mouth, your hands, and do facial expressions that match what your partner's saying." Instant amateur ventriloquist and dummy.

We were forced to stay in the moment. We were forced to be uninhibited. We were forced to say "yes-and" and be willing to laugh at ourselves, our partners, our situations.

Nance had never intended to continue with any follow-up classes that were hawked, but we had such an amazing, creative, hilarious time we got sucked in — so much so we paid for weekly classes for almost a year. Each time we went, it got zanier. We went crazy for the whole enchilada, having found that the exercises and sketches we'd have to tackle, the characters we'd have to inhabit, would rubberize our imaginations and playfulness-glands. And that, of course, was a theme we adored nourishing — and have sustained.

In the process we sometimes "became" weird kids, offbeat adults, or bizarre animals. Now, although we find no need to pretend to be monkeys, we're a lot less sensitive when someone makes one out of us.

Part 25

Fairs 'n' fun

Are you someone who can't pencil in enough fairs on your calendar? We've been to a dozen of our county's five-day annuals. They're earthy enjoyment, with traditional competitions stretching from small-jar preserves to massive blue-ribbon, 4-H cows. They're, at the same time, celebrative, dramatic, splashy, and noisy. Packed with enjoyment for, literally, all generations — and ideal, of course, for a MysteryDate®.

And, normally, easy to get to.

Near a lake and over the hill at the Marin County Civic Center, Big Name entertainers perform in a California tent, their age and talent ofttimes matching that over-the-hill designation. We've over the years nevertheless swayed joyously to nostalgic melodies offered by the likes of Sha Na Na, the Nitty Gritty Dirt Band, and Creedence Clearwater. A lengthy display of fireworks always climaxes the fun (though not, we'd bet, for the ducks, geese, and other aquatic creatures who normally dwell nearby).

State fairs, of course, are cumulative multiplicities of county fairs, often on so much acreage you (or your feet) can't cover it all in a single day. California's, housed near the Sacramento state capitol, attracted us a couple of times.

Fairs, of course, are hotbeds of souvenir collecting. Nancy still cherishes the Borden's Elsie-the-cow mug from the Michigan state fair circa 1948 (even though its handle is long missing, and its insides are caked with unidentifiable substances, so its use now is limited to holding pens that are happy to mark up the bottom when she's not looking after she's forgotten to close them).

What do we remember that was fun at our county's events? Cooking demos, loud barkers, magnificent gardens sand sculptures, myriad technological gadgets and widgets — and mountains and mountains of stuff we had no use for. Nancy says she's unlikely to forget the rubber-ducky races or the 100,000 toothpicks that made up a miniature sculptural display of buildings. Or the people carrying, despite intense summer heat, mammoth stuffed animals they'd won in carnival games.

Yes, ordinary fairs can make enchanting MysteryDates, but those in foreign lands can be even more fun.

Once upon a dream vacation, in Mexico's Yucatan, I created an instant one after a bandana peddler touted me onto a street fair that was going to start in a few minutes.

As Nance and I walked up a rickety flight of tall stairs to a funky restaurant, where we'd be able to see the fair below from "box seats," her eyes nervously fixed on the paint and plaster peeling off the walls. Several large lizards seemed to be leading the way. A dozen small tables were set with chipped China and mangled flatware. But the white linen napkins were clean. We ordered lunch, typical South-of-the-Border fare ("wimpy-American spicy, not Mexican, please," my wife pleaded) and a couple of local beers. Before food or drink arrived, screechy native melodies started to rise from the dusty broken sidewalk below us.

Locals were lining up three and four deep. A funky beauty contest was starting to jell, but a little more exaggerated than home: Contestants' dresses were fussy and exceptionally bright, covered with what Nance playfully called "excessories." Participants' hairdos, sitting extremely high on their teenaged heads, were likewise over the top.

Where we sat, a mariachi band, five lanky, shabbily dressed *señores* started tuning up. We sensed they intended to ignore any outside instrumentalists simply by playing louder.

A mangy stray dog suddenly wandered toward the band and began to howl, head tilted upward toward the standing microphone. He apparently believed the group had booked him as lead singer. "I've gotta get this shot!" I said to my wife, dropping to the floor, adjusting my point-and-shoot digital camera, and sliding on my knees toward the pooch (just like the hero would do in a romcom).

A friendly musician with the best of intentions tried to be a photographer's assistant and — oh, no — turned the animal's head toward me. Miffed, the dog immediately curtailed its canine solo, aimed his head toward the door, and pointed his rear quarters toward me, the would-be photog.

The shot I wanted was gone. But the mental images are forever etched on my cerebral memory chip.

Sometime later we discovered we didn't need to leave the Bay Area to find Latin ambience. All that was required was our presence at a two-day Carnaval. Perfect for a multi-colored MysteryDate.

Neither Nance nor I had ever seen so many feathers — and none of them were on birds. They materialized, rather, on heads, miscellaneous body parts, and especially hands of dancers who stood, sat, and lay on floats, all the while wiggling and wriggling to multiple rhythms played on multiple instruments while parading down the main drag. "These women are outrageously gorgeous," observed my wife. "These women are outrageously gorgeous," I echoed.

The word "sensuous" was an understatement. Virtually every woman, and man, had a fabulous body. And a face to match.

The bands made it impossible to remain a non-moving person, even for those like me who under normal circumstances are rhythmically challenged. In rapid succession, we were treated to musical fusions like Aztec and samba, Brazilian and salsa, sacred dances and blues — plus Bolivian, Cuban and Nicaraguan folk tunes. We stayed a full day, never tiring of the fair, even enthralled with the vendors of junk food and junk trinkets who swayed almost as flamboyantly as the lithe folks on the bandstands and floats. We never tired, either, of the endless frenetic kids who continually cheered, clapped, and stomped.

¡Ay, caramba! Isn't there a Latin community near you that puts on events like that?

And, although we've gone to Carnaval only once, Nance and I have been to local Renaissance faires several times. There, hundreds of merrie-making, festooned 16th century characters wander around, speaking with appropriate if antiquated Olde English accents (some more authentic than others). You'll never know who'll approach you, delight you, engage you, trick you — or invite you to their interactive theater or eatery.

What might you experience? Archery, clothes-washing the Renaissance way, comedians, equestrian competitions, hypnotism, jousting, jugglers, magic, masks, mimes, the pomp and circumstance of Queen Elizabeth and her court — and singing and dancing to music of the era that springs from bona fide instruments of the era. And, yup, you'd be right in style by devouring a colossal turkey leg and drooling down your shirt.

Renaissance or Dickens faires are produced all over the country — in 39 states, at least. Each has its individual characters. charm, flavor, and schedule.

By the way, have you heard the one about the Renaissance monk who had a talking mynah on his head when he stepped into a makeshift pub to get a pint?

Part 26

Love, love, love

When my spouse and I speak of "personal places," we're not referring to private body parts but to locations with special meaning. Frequently romantic, or loving, in their nature.

Your own cache of mental nostalgia unquestionably can generate a made-to-order MysteryDate®. Did you and your partner meet on a subway? At a party? On the job? Did you first kiss in a hollowed-out tree? Whisper on a moonlit beach at midnight? Make love in the back seat of a car or crammed into a phone booth? You needn't wait for an anniversary to commemorate the moment but can pull it into the here-and-now here and now: It's best, we've found, when not expected.

Daters can retrieve indoor memories about events as divergent as shooting billiards or throwing darts, playing Battleship or Backgammon, or burying themselves in raves.

Want to transcend your private recollections? Check out outdoorsy places like Bismarck, North Dakota (which in 2007 broke the record for the most snow angels in one spot: 8,962). There you can hop onto the Lewis & Clark Riverboat that cruises the Missouri, or pause at Buckstop Junction, a reconstructed pioneer village with

20 buildings and a mining camp that depict life as it was before everyone had a video game at their fingertips or, for that matter, running water.

Gee, whiz, I'll bet proverbial dollars to donuts, you can easily find a not-far-away-from-home historic venue that can add to your personalized MysteryDate history.

Love 50 times over

MysteryDates are limited only by your own creative juices. Or the depth of your love. For Nancy's half-century birthday, I held a MysteryDate cake-athon at home.

I lit candles on 50 store-bought cupcakes (baking — or cooking virtually anything, for that matter — has never been a major part of my skill set) and performed a mildly distorted version of "Happy Birthday" (pantomiming the words since my singing voice, she'd convinced me decades ago, resembles a frog with a frog in its throat).

The pièce de résistance came when I handed her 50 symbolic presents, each with 50 parts — an implausible total of 2,500 items. Which weren't as difficult to make as you might think, although it did require a massive expenditure of time and a moderate amount of mental energy.

One gift was composed of 50 gift certificates I'd crayoned (for back-rubbing time, for eating her kind of low-fat food, for me saying "yes" when I wanted to say "no"). A second was a list of 50 things I loved about her. Another included 50 song titles to make her feel warm 'n' fuzzy ("What a Wonderful World," "Good Vibrations," and "Here Comes the Sun"). And yet another featured an itemization of 50 places where we'd had an exceptionally good time together.

On one of my birthday's, Nance's handiwork was much less complex: She hired a friend, a professional comedienne, to show up at my office with her armed with a rubber chicken and jokes.

That kind of foolishness undeniably isn't everyone's cup of Festivi-Tea.

But it's a lot easier to color outside the lines than you might suppose. And you might be surprised to learn how many times (and for how many years) you'll later tell friends about the time that you...

Woody and the woods

The words "gigantic," "majestic," and "tall" take on new nuances when you visit Muir Woods. When we lived together for a short time in Mill Valley, Nance took me on a loving MysteryDate up Mount Tamalpais, driving round and round on scenic roads till we arrived at that wooded national monument. I ended up being awestruck by the "good vibrations" that infuse the park — and impressed by the mélange of visitors encountered as we walked (speaking virtually every language known to humankind).

Let's talk height: The world's tallest trees are coastal redwoods, and Muir Woods is filled with them. It's an old-growth forest with the highest tree measuring 258 feet (approximately the height of a six-foot person stacked head-to-toe 45 times over, according to the official website).

Let's talk old: The average age of the trees in Muir Woods is 600-800 years, with the most seemingly primordial at least 1,200.

Let's talk walking: We stuck to the 1.5 miles of paved road and didn't attempt any of the several nature-trails our first time there together (we've been back more than a dozen times since, each one an utter delight — on an off the so-called beaten track).

The park's website describes what you'll find as an "incredible diversity" of flora and fauna that "can be daunting at times, elusive at other times. The redwoods themselves dominate the scene, but the Steller's jay often steals the show. Ladybugs clustering by the thousands on ancient horsetail ferns boggle the imagination, while the slimy banana slug is able to disgust and fascinate all at once."

Naturalist John Muir, after whom the area was named, was way ahead of the internet and technological revolution when he wrote, "When we try to pick out anything by itself, we find it hitched to everything else in the *universe*."

Spiritual-mystical connections are unavoidable in the woods.

Now, whenever Nance and I meditate, or when we suffer from insomnia, we mentally take ourselves back to the woods and sit on one of the benches there, remembering the sound of the brook running over the rocks and the sound of tranquility.

And we're overcome with love, harmony, peace, and serenity, spiritually not far removed from our first time together as soulmates.

Hidden workplaces

Nance and I love art. And we love to collect it. Especially on the cheap. Once or twice a year, local artists' workplaces, homes, barns, and doors open wide. Art-lovers and curiosity-seekers are invited to walk in and check out their work. Organizers usually label those events Open Studios; I call them potential paths to revelation — and acquisition. And, once again, fun.

The first time we went to that kind of event (which are held in various counties in which and near where we live), I chose — as a MysteryDate, naturally— to see hidden spaces in outlying city districts we didn't know very well. At one of the first stops, an intercom voice invited us in and, after climbing two flights of rickety stairs, we found ourselves walking down a narrow hallway to a miniscule exhibit space where 10 magnificent, huge photographs of African animals greeted us. In other spots, individuals peddled only lavish original oils; still others pushed inexpensive black-and-white postcard reproductions.

We've also discovered massive depictions of muscular men on Harleys, thumb-sized whimsical sculptures, and mixtures of every imaginable media (using clumps of hair or sanitized or still-dirty detritus transformed into a collage or a new art form).

Not long ago, to shake things up a bit, Nance took me on a date to a pier that unveiled a lengthy string of houseboats, and it was mind-blowing how many of them housed open artist studios.

Always, though, whether we buy a 10-buck piece of art or nothing, we seem to end up agreeing with a friend who once declared definitively, "Art is what you hang."

From a cappella to ah, yes

Nance had been listening to a local jazz station decades ago when she first heard "Blackbird" sung a cappella by Bobby McFerrin. And she did something she'd never done before or since — instantly stop what she was doing, drive to a music store and buy the album it was on, then listen to him all the way home. Nowadays, of course, all she'd need do is download it.

She fell in love with McFerrin's talent that day and had an ongoing love affair (from afar) ever since, long before "Don't Worry, Be Happy" made him a household word.

I knew that.

Nance was also a longtime devotee of Garrison Keillor, whose weekly National Public Radio shows had combined elements of satire, storytelling, music, and down-home humor (long before he became a casualty of the #MeToo movement because of fondling accusations). She'd consistently found Keillor's on-air talents irresistible and was a longtime devoted listener. She'd also read several of his books.

I knew that, too.

So, when I learned the two would be appearing together for a live broadcast, I obtained tickets to a rehearsal.

Nance didn't know that.

But the MysteryDate that resulted was, minimally, a 10 for her. Especially when McFerrin speed-sang the entire score from *The Wizard of Oz* in about 10 minutes.

Although my enthusiasm for the show never reached the heights of Nance's, my appreciation for the performers' skills did. And surrendering to one another's wish list is very much an impetus to a shared, loving MysteryDate.

We both know that.

It ain't necessarily no

Even though Nance has seen a handful of operas in New York, Rome, and Vienna, the form is hardly her "drug of choice." But when *Porgy & Bess* came to our stomping grounds, she couldn't wait. After all, the guy who'd written it as an "American folk opera," George Gershwin, has always been tops on her "I-love-him"-list of composers. And although its status had been debated for decades, she truly didn't give a toot if it's called "folk," "opera," "operetta," or something else.

She decided, naturally, to take me on a MysteryDate (presuming that I'd enjoy it a bunch even if my bunch was only half as large as hers).

Tickets were so expensive she ended up buying two in what she termed "the ceiling section" of the cavernous Opera House. All we had to do was extend our fingertips a tad and we could almost dust the ornate chandeliers. My wife couldn't obtain side-by-side seats either; her best choice was to get one behind the other — along with the flimsy hope someone would trade (which, it turned out thankfully, was what happened). If that hadn't worked, she would have had to deal with me literally breathing down her neck in the cramped, highly raked sector.

Bottom line: Despite being concerned about the acoustics that high, not to mention Nance's fears about our ability to see anything, there was absolutely no problem. The performers were amplified flawlessly, and there was a bonus — a gigantic screen hung down in front of the second balcony where we sat. We could watch the singers on stage *or* on the video (with English libretto projected below). Or on both.

We stumbled onto a second bonus, too. An hour before the performance, we heard a free lecture from a docent about the themes, composition, and storyline Gershwin had penned. The woman was well informed, amiable, and couldn't stand still herself when the music about which she was speaking started playing.

I was enraptured by the show. And there's no doubt my partner would do it again in a Gershwin New York minute.

The maneuvering also taught us a lesson we've applied to dozens of MysteryDates since: Don't ever presume you can't get in, can't get tickets, can't do things at the last minute. To upend a Gershwin title, "It Ain't Necessarily No."

Stating the obvious

When the economy — or your family budget — is unusually tight, freebies can be a real blessing. Such events probably exist all around you, though some research may be required. To say that Nance and I love, love, love no-cost excursions is to state the obvious.

A few years ago, as an example, we crossed a bridge to the East Bay to watch a free dragon-boat festival, where thousands of paddlers propelled gorgeous boats in races of all categories. Teamwork. Coordination. Muscles. Cheering. The sound of the coxswain calling out the strokes. Lots to observe; plenty to like. The ancient custom, celebrated in many Asian countries, has expanded into a day (or days) of festivals all over the globe — in Boston, Colorado, Hong Kong, Philadelphia, Toronto, the Twin Cities, and Wisconsin, to mention only a few locales.

Events may feature an activities pavilion, book-signings, face-painters, free games, handmade crafts, international food vendors, lion-dancing, martial arts, prizes for children, stilt-walkers, and hundreds of dragon-boat teams with thousands of boat paddlers. We plan to go again.

Many other recreations in our area don't cost a dime in our neck of the woods — the Cable Car Museum, for example, or the Chinese Cultural Center Gallery, the Fire Department Museum, and the Wells Fargo History Museum.

Prefer live action outdoors to a museum environment? There's no charge to stare at the hundreds of Pier 39 sea lions while they ignore you rather than stare back.

Part 27

Diff'rent strokes

In regard to MysteryDates®, I guess my encouraging "diff'rent strokes for diff'rent folks" implies a multiplicity of undertones and would ultimately depend on what the strokes are and who the "diff'rent folks" refer to, regardless of whether the dates are precisely pre-preplanned or conducted by the seat of your pants or panties.

For example, if you don't like *any* of the trendier sports, all you'd have to do is concoct your own — or participate in one created by someone just as turned off by what everybody else is doing. Know that you can create something unique, or even extreme, and enjoy it. You can use virtually anything as a basis — a grapefruit, a Kindle, a wax candle — to create a sport or a game or an activity that defies ordinary definition. Or, if you're dependent upon someone else's brainstorm, you just might meet someone diff'rent — like Steve Wozniak.

Wozniak, the chunky co-founder of the Apple computer empire, was drawn to a two-wheeled, self-balancing, battery-powered electric vehicle and promptly became a devotee of Segway polo, a faddish team sport that borrowed rules from the two-millennia-old horse polo (which had been the earlier source for the water and bicycle versions as well). Mallets and goals were mainstays of this unique personal-transporter adaptation, with the puck being a Nerf ball with a six-inch diameter.

Teams sprung up, in addition to the United States, in Austria, Germany, New Zealand, Spain, Sweden and Switzerland — with the only thing seemingly missing from the original (which Nancy's grandpappy played) being the horse dung.

Though polo does provide a sliver of exercise, perchance you'd rather focus on *directly* improving your health. Portland, Oregon, to cite but one locale, is a health-conscious city that abounds with gyms, Pilates, and yoga classes. It offers endless ways to strengthen your body (from rock-climbing or skiing to water sports). And, hence, countless ways to set up MysteryDates without your having to reinvent the wheel or anything else.

Meanwhile, for the physically disabled or those who want to watch courageous folks who are, wheelchair races exist in lots of places (topped off by the every-four-years' Summer Paralympics, with 2024's games scheduled for Paris). In a similar vein, Special Olympics encourage participation in year-'round training and competition in a dozen Olympic-style sports. Volunteerism at such events can also offer MysteryDate prospects.

Want to combine charity, hope, *and* sports? The Relay for Life, an annual overnight happening held in a variety of places, does just that. The fund-raising "race," which carries an American Cancer Society imprimatur and celebrates the lives of those who have fought the non-monolithic disease, has team members camp out at a local fairground, park, or high school while taking turns running (or walking) around a track (or pathway).

Through it, more than four million people in more than 20 countries have raised funds for research.

I see no losers in those situations, so each activity must be considered a concrete win-win MysteryDate possibility.

Shaking off the blues

Street fairs, as noted a couple of parts ago, not only feature a vast variety of acts, they draw a mishmash of spectators — another place for "diff'rent" to materialize (and to give off ultra-positive vibes).

I drove Nance to a blues 'n' bar-b-q street fair a couple of towns away from our home. I was sure she'd like the all-day MysteryDate because the music would be as delicious as the eats. Barbecued chicken indeed is high on her Things That Can Make Me Ecstatic list.

We were immediately entertained by a sextet led by an exceptionally gravel-voiced, dark-skinned guy in an exceptionally bright, white suit. The multi-generational audience ranged from toddlers propped up on their fathers' shoulders to oldtimers who sat, stood, strolled, and danced. Several thirtysomethings kept hula-hoops in motion. Three little girls — one bubbly ebony-haired Asian imp, and blue-eyed Caucasian blondes — good-naturedly bumped one another in time to the music while petting our red-haired Golden Retriever.

For the next hour and a half, we tapped our toes until the big ones ached. A minor mass of humanity joined us in devouring the melodies *and* the finger food.

One septuagenarian we later asked her age — who wore a yellow dress and the brightest matching floppy hat we've ever seen — moved more vigorously in her wheelchair than many with two sturdy legs. Another septua- or octogenarian twirled her multi-colored fabric belt while bumping and grinding with sensuality that might have embarrassed her middle-aged children and more than a few onlookers.

All day long, the sauce from pulled-chicken and pork or ribs and tri-tips from California, Mississippi, and Missouri painted endless mouths and hands. Decimated corncobs piled up in trashcans and formed a whacky Modern Art masterpiece. We stayed. We listened. We lazed, taking great pleasure in my easy-to-execute MysteryDate. And then my cell phone jangled. I answered but could barely hear the caller since the new group had turned up its amplifiers to something I dubbed "Let's All Get Rowdy and Deaf."

"Where are you?" asked a longtime friend, Steve Becker. When told, he yelled, "I'm only two blocks from you. I'll be there in a minute." And he was. Unexpectedly, he dragged us away, almost literally: "I'm heading for a 'do,' a block party where there'll be music, food, and upbeat people. And you're coming with me. I won't take 'no' for an answer."

Nance and I looked at each other, and we knew — he'd nag us until we agreed, especially since we had no definitive plans for the next couple of hours and the final band had just taken the stage. So, we followed him. Over the raucous, joyous music, I said directly into my wife's ear: "Since it's a mystery where we're going, and a mystery as to who'll be there, we'll just expand our MysteryDate lexicon and call this a 'Mystery Addendum.'" "Or," added our pal, who'd overheard my loud stage whisper, "maybe 'Mystery Datus Interruptus.'"

What'd we find when we got there? Tons of ukuleles. Tons of Hawaiian shirts and Hawaiian music. And tons of grilled goodies. As well as a horde of happy people who crossed every boundary of age, ethnicity, and instrumental skill level.

Within minutes, folks began strumming or otherwise caressing their four-stringed instruments — acoustic *and* electric. The kanikapila (jam session or sing-along) favored music from the islands. But surprising sound waves of "Over the Rainbow," popularized by the late icon, Israel "Iz" Kamikawiwo'ole, wafted across the nearby pool. As did the French lyrics of "La Vie en Rose."

And we promptly learned the home also had become a joyous blissful mini-fest of hula dancing and pidgin English.

Kites and compost

Has anyone ever told you in an ugly way to go fly a kite? If so, you could easily get the last laugh. If you're traveling abroad and want to set up an exotic MysteryDate, attend the annual Weifang International Kite Festival in that Chinese city known both as the "kite capital of the world" and the birthplace of kites. The fest enthusiastically came back in 2023 after having been quashed by the pandemic for a couple of years.

In the United States, many such festivals are still out of commission — including in Berkeley, where my wife once led me into fields where I could learn just how giant, diminutive, multi-colored, competitive, and octopus-like kites could be, and how science and creative genius could merge and change kite-flying from a solo kiddie affair into an adult amusement.

We all learn about innovation and diff'rentness as soon as we're pushed out of our mother's wombs. And the learning dies only when we do. In between those points, we can endlessly find that we are unique and that many worlds around us are unique. And that, still, we fit into multiple groupings. Some of those thrive online while others exist better on terra firma.

If your comfort zone is spending time in real time and not lost in your computer, your local community can offer ample opportunities. Consider Natick, Massachusetts, where Nance once lived, as a prime example. That town, despite being a quaint place about 15 miles west of Boston populated by only 32,000 people, spearheaded the idea of recycling. With a wee bit of energy expended, it's feasible for you — along with your unsuspecting partner — to learn on a MysteryDate how *your* community, if it doesn't already do it, can collect recyclables at a recycling facility, how you can dispose of trash via a "pay-as-you-throw" program, and how you can pick up environmentally sound ideas about hazardous waste or composting by copying details from the old Natick Green Pages.

Don't care about carbon footprints, energy conservation hybrids, or waste? Well, maybe you have the guts to determine how good, or bad, your singing voice really is? Or your mate's? An open mic probably isn't far from where you bed down.

Maybe you'd rather discover the political bents of your area. You could start a petition and seek signatures together — presuming, of course, that you two agree on whatever you're promoting. And, these days, that you each have multi-layered skin or a bullet-proof vest.

Certifiably odd and eccentric

Interested in spiritual oddities?

If your reply is yes, you might want to take a gander at the Egyptian museum the Rosicrucians built in San Jose.

The sect, formally known as the Ancient and Mystical Order Rosae Crucis (AMORC), broke out of its secret-society cocoon when businessman H. Spencer Lewis went public a touch over a hundred years ago — in 1915. Its website declares its principles are metaphysically oriented but don't constitute a religion, and it points out that "some Rosicrucian members do not subscribe to any specific religious beliefs at all."

The society's block-long headquarters consists of buildings, fountains, rose gardens, and statuary that mimic ancient Egypt conceits. Not to mention a planetarium that promises a glimpse into the future. Followers are contemporary in their thinking, as witnessed by helpful AMORC hints that have appeared on X (formerly Twitter) and Facebook. But Rosicrucian Park, the museum in San Jose, looks backward: It features 4,000 artifacts, including mummies and relics, and highlights a replica of a tomb. It draws more than 100,000 guests annually.

The website, by the way, has included a segment — oddly featuring an animated black scarab that crept across my iMac screen — in honor of cats, which it asserts were first domesticated in Egypt more than 6,000 years ago and treated like royalty.

If you'd rather hop, skip, or jump from antiquity to semi-modern and yet remain firmly in the realm of the diff'rent, simply shift your focus to Emperor Norton I, one of San Francisco's nuttiest in a city long celebrated *and* denigrated for its "nuts and fruits." In September 2023, an alley section of Commercial Street in the Financial District was renamed Emperor Norton Place.

Norton may have been mentally unbalanced. Certifiably eccentric at least. But on Sept. 17, 1859, he instantly became a legend by proclaiming himself emperor of the United States (tacking on "Protector of Mexico" later). That was trailed by a second proclamation by the London native that abolished Congress because it allegedly was "corrupt and fraudulent." A U.S. Army general at the Presidio of San Francisco shortly afterward presented the ex-businessman-landowner with a uniform (which he ultimately wore out).

Norton is most often pictured with his hand on a battered saber, with baggy pants, and a bulging blue naval uniform with tarnished gold-plated epaulets — as well as a beaver hat decorated with a peacock feather. So, it might be fun to create a MysteryDate at one of the sites named after him, such as the Emperor Norton Inn at 615 Post St., a couple of blocks from Union Square and the cable car line. There also are memories of him at his "palace," a rooming house at 624 Commercial St., between Montgomery and Kearny.

During his 21-year "reign," Emperor Norton — who lost a fortune trying to corner the market on Peruvian rice supplies to feed Chinese immigrants — levied taxes and issued worthless local bonds and currency (that some merchants still accepted in trade).

He died in 1880, at age 61, after also having abolished the Democratic and Republican parties because they exhibited excess strife. But Norton-mania may never die.

"His Majesty Norton II, Emperor of Petaluma and Protector of Sonoma County." That's been the alter ego of Tim Hurley, a Kaiser Permanente physician who wrote on his website that he "awakened on New Year's Day 2007 with the realization that he was the successor" to Norton, and "with tongue planted firmly in cheek proclaimed such to the Petaluma City Council in January 2007." His aim wasn't crazy at all — it was to promote the local Committee on the Shelterless.

Anybody out there looking to become Norton III?

Part 28

Home sweet home

"Be it ever so humble, there's no place like home."

That lyric, from a long-forgotten opera titled *Home, Sweet Home*, has been around long enough — more than 150 years, in fact — to become a cliché, needlepoint, and bumper sticker.

I've found that my own humble abode, a modernized hunting lodge that my wife and I had renamed "The Shack," can be a superb location for a MysteryDate®. As can yours.

Nancy once told me to be ready by 6 p.m. I, definitively a Type A individual, *immediately* shaved, showered, and dressed. And waited. Somewhat impatiently, I concede. At 6 o'clock on the dot, our doorbell rang. Standing there were two Type-A friends, arriving for the get-together my partner had coordinated. At 6:04, the bell rang again, and two more guests arrived. That went on until a small but robust group of pals had gathered, all toting food. My wife then disappeared for a few minutes to yank a glut of vittles from their hiding place, our neighbor's fridge. She'd surreptitiously cooked them when I wasn't home.

No special day. No agenda — except to have a home-made, home-style party. And the commute at the end of the evening was our all-time best: We walked down one flight of stairs to our master bedroom.

Not that many days later, Nance informed me we'd have a spur-of-the-moment MysteryDate after lunch. At home, again, but this time with our visiting granddaughter.

Turns out my wife had checked with the local public library and unearthed a slightly battered copy of *Fantasia 2000*, the digitally enhanced version of magical and mythical images Disney artists created to accompany classical melodies — including my favorite segment, Mickey Mouse as "The Sorcerer's Apprentice." In our king-sized bed, Hannah, our non-kissing but affectionate grandchild, tucked her head into my side; my wife warmly held my hand; and my heart skipped a beat or three at a flick I rank equal to Orson Welles' *Citizen Kane* at the top of my list of all-time favorites.

For other home-based entertainments, Nance and I have relied on newer technology, to stream as quick pick-me-ups.

Should we ever start to go stir crazy, a movie date in a town not far from our home (with or without others) can be just the right ticket, our toughest decision being whether to spring for overpriced popcorn and bogus butter. Or go on 50 percent-off Tuesdays.

Pay-it-forward dates also get us out of our home. One recent Thanksgiving, when no family shindig was slated because our kinfolk had fled to "do their own thing," I programmed a date in which we peeled sweet potatoes much of the holiday at a refuge for the homeless.

It took but minutes to realize there are 364 other days a year we could do something similar. In fact, we've already made it a tradition to have Nance regularly play piano at a dining room for poor and elderly people while I ask attendees for requests.

Minimum forethought

Curiosity, conventional wisdom tells us, killed a cat. But Nance and I say that curiosity is a godsend, something that can often lead to an extraordinarily elementary but marvelous MysteryDate.

Such dates can include tons of activities *in or near* your old homestead. Like munching on ham-and-cheese sandwiches on your porch or deck, scooter- or skateboard-riding around the block, eco-touring a neighboring neighborhood, building a safe campfire in nearby hills or mountains. And if you should stray a bit too far out of your comfort zone, we know from the company's ubiquitous TV ads that a nearby Motel 6 will keep its lights on for you.

Always keep in mind, however, that home-styled or quickie dates, regardless how creative or impulsive, are neither panaceas nor magic wands. Relationships, like your favorite rose bushes, need giant doses of cultivating and sunlight. A sense of humor can also help immensely.

Remember, too, that MysteryDates might not be idyllic or effortless for some. Mega-doses of compassion are required, as a for-instance, when planning for the disabled. And since teenagers readily embarrass, you'll need extra care there as well.

Plain ole coupling may, indeed, not work under some circumstances. A collegiate acquaintance recently taught me his peers usually don't date a single member of the opposite sex; they opt instead, he said, for "doing things in groups," preferably inexpensively — or just "hooking-up" for a night. The former can certainly lend itself toward a MysteryDate, the latter not so much.

But if you're in the right mood, I still maintain, MysteryDates can "just happen." Imagine, for example, this real-life scenario: We're both hot messes and decorated from head to toe with shedding-canine hair because I just arrived home with my partner from a pooper-scooper excursion, and I say, "You need to be a little more dressed up. We're going on a MysteryDate — asap." My clothes fly off. So do hers. Two new sets fly on. Her makeup accompanies her in the car, but accessories — despite her usually considering them totally crucial — never get accessorized.

It turns out I've just learned that a friend has some art on display, in a show only minutes from our home. We arrive, tires skidding, because the exhibit only has 20 minutes left before closing. We'd really like to chat with our friend about the exhibit but, a graphic designer informs us, she left half an hour ago because she had a dental appointment. We waste no time lamenting the tête-à-tête that didn't tête. Instead, we munch on the free hors d'oeuvres and race our invisible scooter through the multiple rooms and hallways before breathlessly moving on to a *second* segment of the MysteryDate that I announce halfway through the first — a dark restaurant where a musician couple who also are friends are playing jazz.

The experience clearly proves you don't need to turn "going out" or leaving home into a project akin to the length of time it takes to pen a Ph.D. thesis.

Always, of course, pure inspiration can spur a MysteryDate. One recent weekday when Nance and I were both exhausted and up to our proverbial arses in alligators, I surprised her during one of our noon lunchtime errand runs with an instant meal at our favorite local Thai eatery.

The very next day, as I was having my hair trimmed, she popped her head in, shouted, "MysteryDate," and minutes later led me across the downtown street to my favorite burger joint. Neither date took much forethought. Both worked.

No stilettos, please

Had I suggested to Nance up-front that she'd take to any sport like a kid to cotton candy, she'd have claimed I was wacko. But it turns out she did end up loving our double-date MysteryDate to play bocce, a competition that combines shuffleboard and bowling.

A friend had touted me onto a court only 10 minutes from our home (with a gorgeous rose garden at the entrance) that was built and maintained by a local nonprofit. League regulars played there on teams, but plenty of space remained for casual drop-ins. Since I'd participated in the game only once previously (decades before, while in college), my bocce buddy clued me in again on the details. Our friends had played many times, so they were good at it, and Nance, happily, found it neither complicated to learn nor difficult to appreciate.

We both were thankful we didn't need special clothes, gloves, hats, tight pants, or weird shoes (though soft soles had been advised). And we were tickled to watch one un-briefed middle-aged novice struggling to learn that stiletto heels are *not* recommended.

Since all we really needed to do was show up and toss a little black ball in front of us, Nance and I found it to be a remarkably slow-paced, fun sport. And one she could breezily be a good sport about.

Quashing the qualms

Neighboring states may offer possibilities for MysteryDates distinctly different from those where you live (particularly when buddies' homesteads are there).

For Nance, who doesn't gamble, smoke, drink, or like excessive noise or crowds, Las Vegas is on the absolute tail end of her go-to list. But she does have a lifelong friend who for years lived on the outskirts, so every time she wanted to visit, she had to go through the mental ritual of setting aside all her "don't-likes."

It'd been more than two years since she'd seen her gal-pal when I told my spouse we were going to take a few days away and fly to wherever "there" was, a statement that allowed me to get around having to play the anxiety-packed *packing-for-her* guessing game. Because the gambling hub was nowhere in her consciousness, it wasn't until we neared the boarding gate that she figured out our destination and ascertained we were taking a friendship-flight. That enabled her to quash her qualms about the unknown.

Selfishly speaking, I don't have the same trouble with the city as she, so I was sure there'd be plenty for me to do with her buddy's husband while the women played "remember when." There was.

Then her friend suggested a place all four of us ended up loving: the Liberace Museum. It was an unqualified-10 for my musician wife because of the late performer's glitzy and rare pianos on display. It also was an eye-popping couple of hours for the rest of us because of the larger-than-lifeness of it all (candelabras, diamonds, furs, and rhinestones) that almost required sunglasses to take in — and because we were charmed by the audaciousness of the gaudy outfits, gaudier accessories, and gaudiest cars ever exhibited (more flamboyant even than Elvis').

Although an economic downturn forced the museum's closure in 2010, a new commercial venture, The Liberace Garage, stocked with rhinestone-encrusted pianos, cars he drove onstage, and outrageous costumes launched six years later. It's still open.

Oh yeah, bring on that bling.

Part 29

Birds, butterflies, beasts, bits

It may be easy to find the unusual by examining bird, insect, or plant life on a MysteryDate® in your own backyard — or far, far away across an ocean — without needing a magnifying glass or microscope.

What, for instance, is that plumed creature in the tree right outside your window — a blue grosbeak? A crow? A ruby-crowned kinglet? What, in fact, is that horny robin-lookalike with the white beak and combo white-and-rose belly that's noisily pecking at your windows looking for a partner in mating season?

If you have an interest in counting, learning, watching, or simply appreciating any of those, you can borrow a book from the library, grab your partner for a date, and plan a do-it-yourself outing. Or, if you opt to go beyond the basics, you could set up a session with a few local birders to wander into the woods or onto a body of water somewhere outside your bathtub (and without your pet rubber duckies). Binoculars might help.

It might surprise you to learn that birding is the No. 1 participant sport in America. The Audubon website says so and has quoted the U.S. Fish and Wildlife Service as indicating there are "51.3 million birders in the United States alone."

Across the country, folks have also been counting butterflies. Hey, don't knock it — you don't know when you'll spot a Confused Cloudywing, Great Basin Wood Nymph, or Variable Checkerspot.

The one-day North American Butterfly Association census recruited some 500 teams one year — consisting of greenhorn amateurs as well as longtime lepidopterists (folks who study or collect butterflies and moths). But they were easily overshadowed in the United Kingdom, where the everlasting Brexit tumult didn't deter a recent count by more than 52,000 people detailing more than 580,000 individual butterflies and day-flying moths. At least nobody there is xenophobic about butterflies.

Tangentially, many Americans — including our next-door neighbor — host Monarch butterflies annually (that is, nurture them from when they're eggs until they can be released from human fingertips, a wondrously mind-exploding process).

Fabulous, exotic birds of all kinds and sizes live beyond U.S. borders, of course. Imagine what a great MysteryDate a bird-spotting vacation to Costa Rica or Senegal might entail.

Should you desire to capture more than birds or butterflies with your smart phone or point-and-shoot camera, you might consider a photo safari — to Rwanda, to see gorillas, or Kenya and Tanzania, like we did, to check out all manner of four-footed African creatures. You also can visit Congo centers where they care for bonobos, those pygmy chimpanzees who tend to resolve all their conflicts by having sex.

Just start saving your nickels: None of that's inexpensive.

Sanctuaries also exist in Florida — as well as better-known Thailand facilities — for the care and feeding of endangered African and Asian elephants. At Elephantstay in Ayutthahaya, Thailand, however, you can feed, live among, ride, water and bathe an elephant in the river, allowing you to use a MysteryDate format to "form a personal relationship with your elephant and be part of practical elephant conservation."

Specialized sanctuaries run by the Performing Animal Welfare Society (PAWS) are open to the public only for a limited number of educational events but they, too, are worthy of becoming the foundation of a MysteryDate.

Animals rescued by PAWS live in individually designed enclosures (in Arkansas, California, Florida, and Tennessee) that encourage natural behavior "free from fear, chains and harsh confinement." The creatures — which aren't bred, forced to perform, rented, sold, or traded — may include African lions, bears, black leopards, bobcats, coyotes, elephants, mountain lions, primates, tigers, and wildcats.

Readers of this book who revel in frigid temps may prefer, instead, to embark on an Alaskan dog-sledding adventure with lots of scenery along the way — including a chance to see arctic birds like falcons, golden eagles, ptarmigans, and snowy owls, not to mention caribou, foxes, lynx, mink, moose, otters, ravens, seals, and wolves. From the back of a sled in the tundra you can mush 'n' hush a trained dog on Eskimo trails (and maybe fantasize about taking part in a competitive Iditarod race in the future).

On a vastly different thermometer level, would you rather stay warm and swim with dolphins?

There are tons of places to do that — Belize, California, Florida, Hawaii, and Mexico (Cancun and Cozumel are particularly popular). And the odds are you'll love the intelligent mammals, their noises, and their willingness to interact with bipeds to the degree that you won't want to stop kissing, dancing with, hugging, and rubbing them.

Leftover bits and pieces

Here's a confession: The rest of this section of the book has nothing to do with birds, butterflies, or beasts. Bees, either. And no other critters. The following items are simply *leftovers* — bits and pieces that didn't easily fit comfortably into any other division. Either because they were too tangential or because they would've made a given part too long. Ergo, as I near the end of this book, I figure they can stand as proof that both I and my judgment are human.

Kahlil Gibran, author of *The Prophet*, has been quoted as saying, "In the sweetness of friendship let there be laughter and sharing of pleasures." Nobel Peace Prize winner Elie Wiesel went even further: Friendship, he said, "is never anything but sharing." Sharing a MysteryDate with friends as well as your partner — who in my estimation should be your best friend, your bff — can exponentially increase your delight, I am 110 percent certain.

So...

- Most MysteryDates, with or without amigos, take place on Earth. But I once dove into another dimension, metaphorically speaking. I'd driven Nancy and a couple of buddies to a little theater to see an abstract performance of Hector Berlioz' five-movement *Symphonie Fantastique*. It was hardly a regular orchestral concert, though. For an hour we watched, wide-eyed, through the thick but clear glass of a 500-gallon tank as puppets — *under water* — danced to the music. They were unique creations consisting of bubbles, dyes, feathers, fishing lures, glitter, mirrors, plastic, and other objects. In a previous incarnation on this planet, Nance had been a puppeteer for about 20 years. Still, she'd never experienced anything like this before. Nor had I or our friends. "It's like listening to music with your eyes," Ben Brantley of *The New York Times* had once said of the traveling presentation.

- You don't have to be nuts to enjoy the Nutty Narrows Squirrel Bridges in Longview, Washington. The original, an aluminum piping and fire hose structure, was built for $1,000 in 1963 to stop the animals from being killed while racing across the street below. Because it was rodent-sized, some folks dubbed it the "world's narrowest bridge." Now, though, the town also boasts a 10-foot-tall wooden statue of an acorn-clinging squirrel in the library park *and* several other squirrel spans.

- Several years ago, I planned a secret night out to a comedy club, but days before the MysteryDate-to-be Nance was handed a medical game-changer: She needed surgery on her right foot. At first it looked like her recovery would preempt our evening; happily, however, my wife's doc green-lighted her going. Pushing her temporary wheelchair wasn't that hard, I was happy to find, and the facility had a legislature-mandated ramp to make accessibility easy. Bottom line, so to speak: We laughed our derrieres off.

- Neither Nance nor I had ever been to the two-story,

furniture-and-everything-else-at-basement-prices Ikea store, so I figured it might be fun to spend a morning wandering through the block-long facility even though we weren't in the market for *anything*. I planned the event as part of a two-parter, the second half being to eat lunch at a Korean restaurant. Why? Because I'd somehow erroneously gotten it into my brain that Ikea was a Korean moniker (most likely confusing the store with the car manufacturer Kia). It is, of course, Scandinavian. When we arrived and I read the store's propaganda sheet, I mumbled "Oops!" Nance caught it. "Oops what?" I explained my blunder, and sheepishly revealed that an interconnected lunch wouldn't be part of a themed MysteryDate after all. Anyway, the *smörgåsbord* at the Scandinavian restaurant we ended up at was *läckra* — delicious. We can't say that word with a Korean accent in case you were wondering. And neither of us have yet dared try a MysteryDate at Walmart or Costco.

- Want to plan an extended MysteryDate yet have somebody else make the arrangements? Not only is it possible but hiring a "surprise travel" outfit could allow both your partner *and* you both to be in the dark. About a dozen such tour agencies are thriving in the United States, firms that can let the two of you trip without drugs, stress, or the need to spend hours and hours hassling with details. They *will* disclose the info about where you're going and how you'll get there, but sometimes only 48 hours before you leave — or, in a few cases, at the very last minute. One company, Pack Up + Go, which books only two- or three-day domestic trips, has a slogan almost all the others could echo: "Be adventurous. Be spontaneous. Embrace the unknown." Another, The Vacation Hunt, provides flat-fee trips from three to 14 days with stays at budget-conscious lodging in city centers, but may temper a bit of the suspense by emailing you clues before departure. A Midwestern friend told me she's been quite happy working with two different surprise companies — one for domestic trips, one for international.

- Does your taste run toward the morbid. Try visiting a necropolis, Colma, California, which has fewer than 2,000 living residents and more than 1.5 million dead ones (including Wyatt Earp) — some of them in mass graves. That "City of Souls" or "City of the Silent" (a town, in actuality) long ago banned burials because the cemeteries were out of room and considered a health hazard, and it now boasts the ironic catch phrase, "It's great to be alive in Colma."
- Our longest road trip ever took us through Oregon and Washington, ending up in British Columbia. Everything but the B.C. part, where I'd planned to visit long-time friends in Vancouver, featured impromptu excitement for both of us — we found places to sleep only when we got tired or when it got too dark.

    Our first stop was in California, at Healdsburg. As we approached the motel desk to check in, we heard a loud party. And when the concierge answered our clanging of the bell, we knew we were in for a one-of-a-kind escapade: She announced bluntly, "We're all wasted." Their cannabis harvest had just occurred, so they were celebrating. Inhospitably, they didn't invite us to join them.

At Rainier, Oregon, a diner adjacent to the motel was straight out of The Wonderful World of Elvis. The owners were major fans of The King, so the joint had wall-to-wall paintings of him on velvet, and the counter was jammed with various other Presley paraphernalia (all for sale, needless to say). We bought only dinner. Neither of us was able to explain in the morning why we hadn't slept very well — until we saw where we'd stayed: In the dark, I'd inadvertently chosen a place directly across the street from the Trojan Nuclear Power Plant. The "vibes" we didn't know were there had kept us tossing and turning.

An upscale Bed & Breakfast on Bainbridge Island, near Seattle, was radically different. The view? Water, beach, mountains, and birds. Nance awakened just before sunrise. "First," she later told me, "I sat motionless, staring through the window at the darkness. Very gradually silhouettes formed as the sun rose deliberately, eventually bringing everything into brilliant focus. I was watching what seemed like one magnificent Impressionist painting after another emerging in slow motion. I didn't move a muscle. I've never been so grateful for insomnia."

Despite knowing that would be tough to beat, I decided to undertake a mystery drive up the Rogue River, a protected wildlife area where we watched bald eagles hunt and soar and heard tales of beavers and black bears and river otters, mink, newts, and gray foxes (though we didn't see even one of those critters). We did pledge to each other to come back and stay where visitors camp, take all kinds of boat trips, and see the wildlife close-up. Someday…

Part 30

Mysteries

Although MysteryDates® might not always be effortless, nearly everyone — because they typically are jam-packed with slapstick and other humor — can enjoy murder-mystery dinners. Entrepreneurs in many cities across the land offer them. And what, I ask rhetorically, could be a more fitting setting for a MysteryDate?

The one Nancy scheduled had urged guests to come prepared with a detective name that would be put on a tag. Since she was bringing a momentarily-in-the-dark me, she secretly chose my moniker — and, since we're both fans of alliteration, she dubbed me Claude Clueless (while choosing the more grounded Gloria Gumshoe for herself).

Promotional materials accurately described what was to come: "A shriek is heard, death is dealt, bodies fall, and both the innocent and the guilty are gathered to ferret out suspects." The evening we attended, eight actor-singers portrayed characters in a performance that resembled a melodramatic TV reality show; they continually feigned shock and awe in various degrees of hamminess. But fun it was.

Because it sounds gimmicky as Hades to conjure up a MysteryDate with the word "mystery" attached, finding a pair that could cheerfully send us day-tripping — the Winchester Mystery House and the Mystery Spot — gave us both as much satisfaction as solving an Agatha Christie whodunnit.

The former, a 160-room Victorian house on nine acres in San Jose, is sort of an architectural Frankenstein's monster created by Sarah L. Winchester, wife of the son of the guy whose name is synonymous with repeating rifles. After her infant daughter, Annie, and hubby, William, both died unexpectedly, she consulted a medium and was informed that the spirit world was displeased because many of its inhabitants had been killed by the "Gun that Won the West." The rent-a-psychic claimed phantoms were seeking revenge, and suggested she move from New Haven, Connecticut, to the west and build a house in which the ghosts could find peace. He also told her she couldn't ever stop expanding the house because when the workmen stopped, she'd die.

Browbeaten, Sarah followed the spiritualist's directions, buying an eight-room farmhouse in 1884 and spending $5.5 million of her $20 million inheritance on the project. The carpenters (22 of them at a clip) were kept busy 24/7 for 38 years (partially because she constantly changed the blueprints). The work kept up her spirits, though. She also kept the ghostly spirits busy with nightly séances. Although she didn't sleep in the same bedroom two nights in a row, she lived in the mansion until her death in 1922 at age 85 (except for a brief stint after the 1906 quake, which took the house down to four stories from seven).

Eventually, construction resulted in more than 2,000 doors and five times that many windows. Some of those openings and stairways lead to twisting-and-turning corridors that go nowhere. Or to sheer drops. There are other oddities as well. A window in the floor. Hallways that dwindle into crawl space. Trap doors. A chimney that doesn't reach the roof. Upside down posts. If you go, look for designs with 13s, spider webs, and daisies. They're everywhere.

The Winchester House, haunted or not, may be the ultimate Silicon Valley tourist snare, replete with hidden doorways and phony passageways that tour guides will be happy to show you. Unfortunately, anyone confined to a wheelchair can't make it through the labyrinth (the house pre-dates the 1990's Americans with Disabilities Act).

Since the house has been opened to the public, there have been reports of mysterious footsteps, banging doors, voices coming from nowhere, weird moving lights, and doorknobs that turn without help. So, keep at least one eye out for the paranormal.

If you can't make it there in person, you still might want to check out *Winchester*, a 2018 Helen Mirren-starring film. Yes, watching that mediocre flick could be a MysteryDate unto itself — and a mystery: Why did you bother in the first place?

In the meantime, the Mystery Spot, a circular hillside area about 150-feet in diameter discovered in 1939 by some surveyors, is all about emptiness — and, perhaps, natural phenomena that repeal the laws of gravity and physics. There, in Santa Cruz, people apparently can walk up walls or, for the timid, watch water flow upwards.

What can visitors experience? Well, a small shack sits over a vortex that makes billiard balls roll uphill, and adult

Homo sapiens look like they're standing at odd angles. Some claim that buried within are UFOs that altered the laws of gravity. A handful of analysts theorize that leaking carbon dioxide causes the effects, but others believe they stem from changes in the ozone layer. Skeptics insist what you see on a 45-minute tour is all optical illusions created by business folk desirous of altering the contents of your wallets.

Blowing Rock, North Carolina, offers a similar attraction, Mystery Hill, with a "crooked house" that also apparently defies gravity. Balls and water roll uphill, and folks stand at an angle of 45 degrees. The entertainment center includes a "hall of mystery" that contains a "spooky spigot," a "magic light bulb," and a "flying mirror."

Unsolved, unresolved mysteries? Dubious. Good business? Undoubtedly.

Speaking of enjoying good business, the Ghost Baby in Cincinnati does just that with regularity, thank you very much. It's a unique bar that draws crowds because of its moody lighting, cocktails, and music *and* because it's in tunnels four stories underground that had been used by a brewing company until the 1850s. Some fearful folks claim to have heard "ghostly sounds" in some of its rooms.

Riddle, mystery, or enigma?

MysteryDates can be stimulating if only because they involve the unknown. But even if you can correctly project how a given date will turn out, you may believe as writer Anais Nin did: "The possession of knowledge does not kill the sense of wonder and mystery. There is always more mystery."

While researching this volume, I became more than a little enthused thinking about the origin of the Middle

English word "mystery." It dates to the early 1300s but stems from both ancient Latin and Greek references to a hidden or secret thing, and allusions to closed eyes and lips.

Anyway, to provide an inside-joke overlay on a MysteryDate, why not rent or purchase some books or games with "mystery" in the title for dual reading — or old *Mystery Theater* radio shows? Or have a buddy mysteriously come up with a "double-date MysteryDate" by making all the arrangements with you and your partner both in the dark.

From a list of possibilities as long as traffic jams at major malls on Black Friday, you alternatively could:

- Sign up you and your mate to become mystery shoppers, to buy goods in a store and report to management who's doing things right and who isn't. Beware, though, of mysterious scammers trying to rip off your personal data before you start.
- Pretend you're a pre-pubescent girl and play the 1965 Milton Bradley "Classic Mystery Date" board (and card) game. Reissued several times (last in 2009, with a *High School Musical 3* update), it focuses on dancing, bowling, beach, and skiing dates.
- Stream a modern techno-thriller laced with computer graphics, a classic Edgar Alan Poe tale, or a lighthearted Inspector Clouseau caper — and invite a bunch of mystery-lovers over to your place to figure out the ending. Or to laugh. And possibly to eat mystery food brought by each guest and guess its ingredients.
- Explore the mysteries of "other worlds" — Earth itself, its skies or oceans, science or the unknown, Area 51 or various aliens, or phantoms or other

supernatural beings or happenings.
- Visit sites of long-lived, true mysteries (such as the Bermuda Triangle section of the North Atlantic, where planes and ships have vanished suddenly).
- Establish a small ongoing murder-mystery club with your goal being regularly or erratically scheduled dates for you, your partner, and another couple.
- Check out the Wavertree Playground, known in the Liverpool area as The Mystery, a public area financed by a mysterious anonymous donor in the United Kingdom in 1895 who gave the city 108 acres of land. The real mystery is why the nickname stuck.
- Jointly read the *Mystery Date* e-book by Denise Little that contains 17 stories of blind dates (including such personalities as Shakespeare and Zeus). Or dig up and play a 2001 CD by Mystery Date (an a cappella quartet once known as Sons and Lovers) that offers sophisticated, jazzy harmonies.
- Search libraries, archives, retail stores, or online sources for a new or used video or DVD copy of the 98-minute, 1991 MysteryDate-at-home romantic-comedy, *Mystery Date*, starring an incredibly young Ethan Hawke in a farce about mistaken identity and a pair of corpses in a car trunk.
- Stay-at-homers can spend an evening listening and re-listening (with all appropriate nostalgia), to the *Magical Mystery Tour*, an 11-track psychedelic rock LP recorded by the Beatles back in 1967.

As you can see, MysteryDates can be uncomplicated, or as complex as Winston Churchill described Russia: "A riddle wrapped in a mystery inside an enigma."

Part 31

Afterword

The idea of dating, despite conventional wisdom, mythology, or scrawls on cave walls, doesn't go back to the Neanderthals, the ancient Chinese, Greeks, or Hebrews. It's a 20th century phenomenon, one that broke the back of the arranged-marriages concept.

If we look in the rear-view mirror as recently as colonial America, we find romance didn't define wedlock as much as did the idea of men wanting wives who'd bear children to help work the land. More than a few Third World countries today still see it that way. In the United States, however, romantic love (and, eventually, casual sex) replaced the more formal courtship in which women welcomed the attention of suitors.

Chaperones disappeared as a social necessity. Boy-girl outings with fewer rules and regulations temporarily became a comparatively painless substitution. Dating swiftly removed relationships from the parlor, morphing them into what was labeled "going out." And "out," logically, was translated as "anywhere but home."

Going to motion pictures and dancing became trendy forms of dating, each ramping up levels of intimacy and physical contact. The 1920s and its petting parties then acted as forerunners of a new freedom that would be displayed by servicemen returning from World War II. Suddenly, during the 1960s, both male and female genders extended their liberties when drugs and rock 'n' roll easily trickled onto or off tongues. The Pill and its adjunct Sexual Revolution spearheaded the changes. Dating restrictions became non-existent.

For a while.

Only a few decades later, along with the proliferation of workspace cubicles, closeness had dissipated. Regular dating grew less appealing in the face of social networking and speed-drooling. Intimacy was supplanted by text-messaging and "friends with benefits."

The pandemic, of course, fostered sheltering in place and isolation, situations that in turn created a mentality almost entirely anathema to dating. Much of that attitude persisted even after restrictions about leaving home and mask-wearing were lifted.

In hopes of bringing back the best of yesteryear, I've now emphasized the idea of MysteryDates®, where touching psychologically and physically isn't merely desirable but a prerequisite, where the only cap (other than a creator's imagination) is the willingness of participants to join in. And, I suppose, a willingness to do a little work — such as what Nancy managed for my 65th birthday.

Several months before that calendar date, Nancy asked how I'd like to mark it. "With a phalanx of ravishingly beautiful dancing girls," I answered without hesitation, 1,000 percent flippantly.

True to form, my wife secretly sought comic relief from half a dozen of my fellow workers.

When the festive day arrived, she provided each with a snippet of a costume from a different country, and supplied, thanks to Google, the way to say "happy birthday" in the appropriate language.

And, in her workplace a few blocks from mine, she'd dressed one of my pals — a 6-foot, 3-inch dude — in a black nightgown, lacy gloves, and hooker-like makeup. His clunky combat boots made the outfit even more bizarre, even funnier. Half an hour later the big guy, Josh Brandt, read French poetry to me, the birthday boy, while simulating a lap dance.

Unsurprisingly, not a single person had paid any attention as he paraded through the streets of San Francisco — even considering that Nance was walking next to him in a kimono with her hair in a bun held together with forks and chopsticks.

That kind of foolishness undeniably aren't everyone's cup of any kind of tea.

But it's a lot easier to color outside the lines than you might suppose. And you might be surprised to learn how many times (and for how many years) you'll tell friends about the time that you...

Trust and acceptance

This volume, it should be evident, is a guidebook, not a magic bullet or magic formula, based on years of experiences (and voluminous research), geared toward helping you manifest my concept.

Because so much more than MysteryDates are needed for a healthy relationship, however, I'll summarize your need to *also* embrace the following with your partner:

- GOOD COMMUNICATIONS. It's helpful to present *all* the facts and not edit out what might be troublesome or unpleasant.

- TRUST. It's useful to eliminate all lies, even little white ones, even lies of omission.
- HABITUATED RITUALS. Every morning Nance and I spend 10 intimate minutes together — without sex. Sometimes we're silent and just hold hands; sometimes we tell the other person what we love about him or her, or list five to 15 behaviors we are grateful for, or whatever wholly positive list we've created that day (we recently spent our time on what we like about our environment, on what we love about our pooch, on how our friends have helped us). Every a.m. one of us will say, "I love you," with the heartfelt response being "I love you." No "too" is added. We also start our days by dipping into a book of love quotes, each of us in succession opening it randomly and reading one aloud. Each morning, in addition, we ask each other this question: "What can I do for you today?" Our answers have ranged from "Be compassionate, I'm fragile because..." to the more often "Nothing special but thanks for asking." Nance plays a mini-concert on the piano for me each morning, when the sun isn't in her eyes — or, if it is, in the afternoon or evening: Two songs she randomly selects, followed by "My Funny Valentine," *our* song. Then, at bedtime, both of us say, and mean it, "Today's been the best possible day we could have had," regardless of what difficulties we encountered at any part of it.
- EXCHANGE. Nance and I choose to show our affection in a mass of *other* ways (except once in a great while), but you and your partner may be big gift-givers. Presents, for special days or "just-because" days, can run the gamut from bling or a

new car to the trimming of wiry eyebrows.
- ACCEPTANCE. We've found it crucial to take each other "as is," warts, doots, wrinkles, sagging skin, and varicose veins included. That's quite different than our early days together when, because we both were only children and used to getting our own way, we disagreed and argued a lot while jockeying for position.

Your bottom line is all in your hands — and, as I've indicated repeatedly, your imagination.

This, then, is the end.

I'm done, partially because I've said what I have to say, partially because I'm pushing the clock: Nance and I are going out on yet another sizzling, spontaneous, and special MysteryDate in just a few minutes.

Thanks

This MysteryDates® book could not have been completed without the help of the following people, each of whom I thank profusely:

- Nancy Fox, my wife, partner, friend, companion, lover, editor, and frequent collaborator whose support has been endless (except for the 17 times when we were squabbling).

- Joe Marciniak, the artist who perfectly superimposed my mug and Nancy's under the Sherlock Holmes deerstalker caps on the front cover that helped tempt you to pick up this volume.

- Ruth Schwartz, who midwifed MysteryDates so it became more than just a wannabe manuscript.

- Abby Everson, whose legal expertise helped me successfully navigate the deep waters of federal government regulations about service marks.

- Steve Cook and Wayne Heuring, whose editing advice helped punch up my prose, syntax, and continuity (and eliminate all those typos that might have flummoxed you).

- And Kismet, our purebred rescue mutt who rested at my feet for countless hours while I toiled on this volume.

Woody Weingarten, a bio

I, Woody Weingarten, author of this MysteryDates® book, can't remember a time when I couldn't talk or play with words. My first poem was published in high school but when my hormones told me I was an adult, I decided I'd rather eat than write rhymes.

I've been professionally using words — big, small and hyphenated, with lots of dashes and semi-colons — since beginning my career as a journalist in New York City more than 65 years ago.

In addition to writing a national column plus arts and entertainment reviews, I've edited daily and weekly newspapers in California, New Jersey, New York, and Pennsylvania. I even published a couple of my own papers in Clearwater, Florida.

With a bunch of writing awards and two lines of snappy greeting cards under my belt, along with 20 extra pounds abetted by the pandemic, I published *The Roving I*, a collection of 70 newspaper columns I'd penned over more than a decade, and a whimsical children's book, *Grampy and His Fairyzona Playmates*, co-authored by my then eight-year-old granddaughter, Hannah Schifrin, 70 years my junior. Earlier, I'd written a book, *Rollercoaster: How a man can survive his partner's breast cancer*, which depicts my emotional journey as a male caregiver through the disease that my wife, Nancy Fox, quashed for more than a quarter of a century.

Nance and I, not incidentally, have been concocting MysteryDates for 35 years. Although Covid brought those inventions to an abrupt temporary halt, we're back in high gear and don't plan to stop anytime soon.

More Woody Weingarten books

If you liked *MysteryDates®*, check out the three previous books I've written: *The Roving I: Collected columns, wit, wisdom, and self-exposure of Woody Weingarten*; *Grampy and His Fairyzona Playmates*; and *Rollercoaster: How a man can survive his partner's breast cancer*.

The Roving I: Collected columns, wit, wisdom, and self-exposure of Woody Weingarten anthologizes 70 of my own favorite first-person essays. My memories include my partner earning a slot in my Little Black Book, a friend turning Parkinson's Disease into an asset, a woman carrying her sister's "miracle baby" inside her for nine months, a Cambodian slave-labor camp escapee becoming a successful U.S. entrepreneur, and Robin Williams transforming himself into a talking vagina.

Grampy and His Fairyzona Playmates, which was co-written with my granddaughter, Hannah Schifrin, 70 years my junior, offers a whimsical but educational tale for children aged 6 to 10. The fantasy showcases Grandpa Graybeard, a sorcerer who frequently must get his granddaughter Lily and her best friend Penny out of trouble when the two eight-year-old fairies mess up their magic spells. Their misadventures become great fun for all three, *and* for young readers who love to let their imaginations run wild.

Rollercoaster: How a man can survive his partner's breast cancer provides a comprehensive memoir-chronicle (a love story), and a guide to scientific research, meds, and where to get help. It shows how my wife, Nancy Fox, and I coped with the disease, its treatments, and its aftermath — and how readers can as well. Almost 250,000 new breast cancer cases are diagnosed annually. Male caregivers (husbands, boyfriends, fathers, sons, and brothers) typically become a forgotten part of the equation. Yet they too, need support. *Rollercoaster* can help provide it to them — as well as to female caregivers, and to patients themselves. I, a prize-winning writer who became a breast cancer expert reluctantly, now unflinchingly share what I've learned from personal experience and from leading a weekly male partners' group for almost three decades.

All three books I wrote were published by VitalityPress.

More information on the books and me can be found at woodyweingarten.com or vitalitypress.com.

www.ingramcontent.com/pod-product-compliance
Lightning Source LLC
Chambersburg PA
CBHW070536010526
44118CB00012B/1148